How to Survive
a Training
Assignment

How to Survive a Training Assignment

A Practical Guide for the New, Part-time or Temporary Trainer

STEVEN K. ELLIS

ADDISON-WESLEY PUBLISHING COMPANY INC.
Reading, Massachusetts   Menlo Park, California
New York   Don Mills, Ontario   Wokingham, England
Amsterdam   Bonn   Paris   Milan   Madrid   Sydney
Singapore   Tokyo   Seoul   Taipei   Mexico City   San Juan

The publisher offers discounts on this book when ordered in quantity for special sales. For more information please contact:
Corporate & Professional Publishing Group
Addison-Wesley Publishing Company
Route 128
Reading, Massachusetts 01867

Library of Congress Cataloging-in-Publication Data

Ellis, Steven K.
How to survive a training assignment: a practical guide for the new, part-time or temporary trainer/Steven K. Ellis.
p. cm.
ISBN 0-201-06647-5
1. Employees, Training of—Handbooks, manuals, etc. I. Title.
HF5549.5.T7E43 1988 658.3'124—dc19 87-29954

Cover design by Louise Noble
Text design by Carson Design
Set in 11 point Trump Medieval by Ampersand Publisher
Services, Inc., Rutland, VT

ISBN 0-201-06647-5

8 9 10 11 12 13 14 –DO– 9796959493
Eighth printing March 1993

Contents

	Page
Editorial Note	vii
Preface	ix
Chapter 1 Working with Adult Learners	3
☐ Characteristics of Adult Learners	4
☐ Expectations of Adult Learners	6
☐ Barriers to Learning	7
Chapter 2 The "Mystery" of Instructional Objectives	15
☐ The Importance of Instructional Objectives	16
☐ Tips for Creating Instructional Objectives	17
Chapter 3 Designing the Training Program	21
☐ Factors Affecting Program Design	22
☐ Guidelines for Program Design	26
Chapter 4 Instructional Techniques	31
☐ Presentation Technique	32
☐ Question-and-Answer Discussion Technique	40
☐ Small-Group Discussion Technique	49
☐ Demonstration/Practice Technique	58
☐ Case-Study Technique	64
☐ Review Technique	72
Chapter 5 Visual Aids	79
☐ Factors in Selecting Visual Aids	80
☐ Types of Visual Aids	82
☐ Using Visual Aids Effectively	87

Chapter 6 Building an Effective Lesson Plan   91
    ☐ Types of Lesson Plans   93
    ☐ Practice and Evaluation   99
    ☐ Organizing the Lesson-Plan Sequence   100

Chapter 7 Tips for Making Effective Presentations   103
    ☐ Keys to Effective Presentations   106

Chapter 8 Using Subject-Matter Resources   115
    ☐ Ways to Use Subject-Matter Resources   116
    ☐ Identifying and Securing the Assistance
      of the SMR   117
    ☐ Following Up the Training Session   119

Chapter 9 Evaluation and Feedback   123
    ☐ Ways to Evaluate a Program   124
    ☐ Ways to Take Corrective Action   129
    ☐ Ways to Give Constructive Feedback   133

Summary   135

Additional References and Materials   139

Checklists and Worksheets for Effective Instructional
Preparation   143

Editorial Note

Since trainers in business today are both male and female, it is important to recognize both genders in a text such as this. To do this while not burdening the reader with cumbersome wording, we have minimized the use of "he or she" references. Instead, the approach in the text is to alternate masculine and feminine pronoun references to achieve an overall balance and to reflect real-world experiences. We think this adequately addresses the issue and benefits our readers.

Preface

In the corporate training environment there are essentially two kinds of trainers. There are the full-time professional trainers who have studied training-program development and group-process theories and techniques. Then there are the part-time trainers who are given the task of training others as an additional responsibility beyond the typical job tasks they must perform daily. This text is designed for the latter group of individuals.

The part-time trainer is usually a person who has demonstrated technical proficiency in a given area and who is then subsequently asked to pass on this technical knowledge and skill to others. Managers almost naturally assume that if a person knows information in detail, he or she can be a good trainer and communicator. Unfortunately, this is not always the case.

Rarely has the "supertechnician" had the benefit of studying group-process concepts, been able to work with other skilled instructors to observe how they manage a training session, had the opportunity to have his or her training session videotaped and critiqued by peers, been given much time to learn different types of instructional techniques, or had the opportunity to conduct training sessions with some degree of frequency so that past successes and shortcomings remain fresh in his or her mind.

If you fall into this technician-turned-trainer category, this text is designed to fill some of these gaps. Its purpose is to provide you, the part-time trainer, with some "survival information" that will help you prepare for and facilitate the majority of training situations you are most likely to encounter. No text, however, can substitute for actual training experience in the classroom environment.

In this text you will be provided tips regarding

- [ ] the nature of the adult learner and why the knowledge of these characteristics is important to you when designing, developing, and facilitating a training session;
- [ ] instructional objectives and why they are important;
- [ ] some of the primary instructional techniques you can use—either by themselves or in combination with others—in order to effectively facilitate virtually any training session;
- [ ] visual aids you can use to support your training efforts;
- [ ] criteria you should consider when putting together a lesson plan;
- [ ] the effect verbal and nonverbal actions can have on how well a presentation is received by the audience;
- [ ] how you can identify and secure the assistance of other subject-matter resources to aid in the development and/or facilitation of a training program;
- [ ] how a training program's effectiveness can be evaluated and how feedback can be provided to individuals who fall below the desired learning-competency level.

In addition, the text provides a handy checklist which you can use to assure yourself that all the major training concerns involved with planning, organizing, and/or conducting an on-site or off-site training session have been considered.

This text is not, nor was it designed to be, a totally definitive treatise on everything you need to know about training. Instead, it seeks only to provide fundamental tips and ideas about how a training session should be effectively designed and conducted.

The "secret" to being an effective trainer is knowing your material, knowing the audience to whom you are speaking, being a good communicator, and having a keen ability to listen. To become even better requires a willingness to experiment with new training approaches, to solicit feedback on how well your session was received, and to listen to the feedback and change those personal traits and/or instructional techniques that were not effective.

Learning should be an enjoyable experience for the student. It is your responsibility to help achieve this level of excitement by providing the right environment within which this learning can take place effectively. By knowing the audience, understanding the fundamentals of how various instructional techniques can be used effectively, knowing when and how to use audiovisual aids, recognizing the value of effective presentation skills and soliciting (and listening to) student feedback, you can establish this environment. An added benefit is that by knowing and applying these key fundamentals, you will find training can also be an enjoyable working (and learning) experience for you as well.

This text attempts to provide insight into these training fundamentals. The rest is up to you—to experiment, to practice, and to evaluate. Enjoy!

CHARACTERISTICS OF ADULT LEARNERS

- Pursue training with a sense of purpose
- Have some relevant knowledge or skill
- Are motivated by goals
- Want training to relate to the real world
- Need to have theory immediately applied to practice

WHAT PREVENTS ADULTS FROM LEARNING

- Being afraid of criticism
- Forgetting how to learn and take tests
- Negative memories of other training experiences
- Competing priorities

WHAT WORKS BEST IN TRAINING

- True-to-life examples and data
- Having individuals share with trainees
- Real-world case studies

WORKING WITH
ADULT LEARNERS

You've just been handed a training assignment, and you are probably thinking, How am I going to pull this off? What am I going to do so I will be able to teach the people what they need to learn? To calm your anxieties, you probably will think back to how you were taught when you were in school. We all have memories, fond or otherwise, of the learning techniques that our teachers used during our years of formal schooling, whether at the grammar school or postgraduate level. When we find ourselves having to train other people, we tend to draw on these earlier learning experiences as we decide how to teach our material.

We need to remember, however, that the techniques that were acceptable to us may not work with others. Why does this happen? What has changed? As an academic student, we had different motivations for learning than we have now as adults, and it is the recognition of these differences that must be taken into consideration when designing a training program for an adult audience. We want to be able to produce consistently positive training results, but this will not be possible unless we clearly understand when and why one instructional technique is more effective than another.

This chapter deals with some of the qualities and mind-sets of the adult learner and what you, as a trainer, should do to maximize the learning experience of your audience. Later chapters contain information on the specific instructional techniques.

Characteristics of Adult Learners

First, it is important to realize how adult learners differ from academic learners. An academic learner has one main short-term goal: to fulfill the educational requirements for an academic degree or for continued academic advancement. Rarely does this learning apply to the specific and immediate challenges of the workplace.

In contrast, adult learners want to obtain knowledge and skills that they can apply to a clearly defined challenge or demand in their work. Their time is too precious to spend on training that does not relate immediately or in the near future to their employment. In business training you will most likely meet adult learners who have the characteristics discussed in the following sections.

SENSE OF DIRECTION

Probably the biggest educational motivator of adult learners is their confidence that the knowledge or skill development they are pursuing will apply to a specific need they have for professional growth. Individuals in the business world tend to have a better sense than academic learners of the direction they want to move in. As a result, their pursuit of necessary training programs and materials is more focused. These adult learners have a strong desire to attend appropriate courses or read relevant educational material. In the academic environment students choose the courses they need to graduate to the next level rather than courses they think will be professionally interesting and rewarding.

BASE OF EXPERIENCE

Adult learners come into a training situation with some relevant knowledge or skill. Because of this, they have the opportunity to learn from the experiences of others in the group. They can build upon and relate their own trials and tribulations. In the academic setting the experiences students bring to the group are very limited and too general to be of value to the other students. In addition, adults generally learn more from their peers than they do from an outside party (such as a corporate trainer). Therefore, to be most successful, the training session should provide as many opportunities as possible for participants to draw upon these peer-group learning experiences.

GOAL ORIENTATION

Individuals in the business world—especially those in medium to large organizations—know that their performance will be evaluated. They also realize that the evaluation can affect their opportunities for advancement. People who aspire to higher positions are therefore motivated to prepare themselves. They hope that when a desired position becomes vacant, their work efforts, performance results, and training experiences will give them an edge over their competitors. Thus, adult learners will seek courses congruent with their career plans and will work hard to get as much as they can out of these learning experiences.

Expectations of Adult Learners

REAL-WORLD APPLICATION

Because adult learners are motivated to attend training sessions in order to achieve a short- or long-range goal, they want the training session to deal with problems and/or situations that are directly related to their business environments. So the more closely related you can make the subject material to the work your trainees are actually performing, the greater chance that they will perceive your session as useful.

IMMEDIATE APPLICATION OF THEORY TO PRACTICE

In addition to being relevant to the real-world environment, the information you present should also—to the greatest extent possible—be structured so the participants can easily and immediately apply the theory to practical situations. In this way, the adult learners will have prompt feedback on whether they have properly interpreted how these concepts can be applied and can realize the effects and consequences of their actions. The latter can be especially enlightening when learners are put into interactive roles where they can practice, in a safe classroom environment, techniques for conducting an effective job interview, putting data into a computer, handling disciplinary problems of subordinates, or similar situations.

Training sessions that take place off the job are especially helpful for applying theory to practice because they give participants a chance to experiment with new techniques and to practice in a nonthreatening environment what they have learned. By practicing away from their work stations, participants will not be afraid that errors in execution will have a detrimental effect on their performance evaluation and on their chances for professional advancement.

6

Barriers to Learning

FEAR OF CRITICISM FROM MANAGERS AND PEERS

Perhaps the greatest fear adult learners have of training is that they will give a negative impression to their managers and peers. This leads to the training participants' fear that other people might criticize their ability to perform their job. This is especially true for a worker who has been on the job for a number of years and who has been viewed, either formally or informally, as the key resource person in the department or unit. In fact, this fear can be very strong and may manifest itself in the form of various behaviors. For example, you may find that some of the more experienced individuals who have been asked to attend a training session are usually absent because of illness or an "important" meeting. Or they may attend but not participate. Unfortunately, for true peer-group learning to be maximized, this kind of person needs to participate. Should you encounter this situation, you may want to try

- □ asking the individual to attend the training session in the role of a subject-matter resource (this is described in greater detail in chapter 8).

- □ securing this individual's assistance in developing and/or reviewing case studies, illustrative examples, and so forth.

- □ using this individual as a springboard with whom you can discuss your lesson plan and get her ideas about the appropriateness and accuracy of your material, as well as her feedback on how she might handle different kinds of situations.

SPAN OF TIME SINCE LAST FORMAL LEARNING SESSION

For many adults, a long time has passed since they were last involved in a formal training program. Activities such as prework, homework, postsession assignments, test taking, and going through in-class exercises are no longer recent experiences. People forget how they used to handle these activities most efficiently and therefore need time, and perhaps help, to reacclimate themselves to these tasks. Therefore, you should try to determine in advance as much as you can about the people you will be training so that you will be able to structure the learning experiences accordingly.

For example, if your trainees are corporate interns who are just starting with the company, you can be assured that they have some level of recent experience in a training environment. On the other hand, if your audience is comprised of people who have been with the company for several years, the time since their last training experience may vary widely. Therefore, you may want to determine through an informal survey or through research of existing personnel and/or training records what degrees or professional certificates they have attained and when they received these honors, other training programs in which they have participated, when these were completed, and so forth.

Where there has been recent training experience, you will probably have success with virtually any type of training work activity. However, the longer people have been away from training, the more they have to be eased into the different types of activities. In the beginning avoid homework, complex case studies, and exams that require a high degree of memory skills. Instead, use in-class exercises followed by immediate discussion and feedback. Once this comfort level has been achieved, you can work more complex activities into the curriculum.

MEMORIES OF EARLIER TRAINING EXPERIENCES

Most people can recall some learning experience that bothered them deeply. For some people taking a test was unpleasant. Other people had a negative experience when appearing on videotape, participating in a role play, or acting as a group spokesperson. An invitation to participate in a training session will almost certainly trigger some of these negative memories in your students. To be an effective facilitator, you will need to probe for these concerns throughout the training session and attempt to minimize their impact.

Some ways you may attempt to uncover and/or minimize these fears are to

☐ ask the group whether anyone strongly objects to being on videotape. If someone does, exclude them from a videotaped session. Perhaps being audiotaped might be an acceptable substitution.

☐ minimize people's fears of tests by explaining how the tests are structured and emphasizing that all results will remain strictly confidential. Allowing people adequate time to prepare for the test will also calm some uneasiness, as will having people work as a team in preparing for it.

☐ provide opportunities for remedial work for those who do not grasp the concepts as quickly as others.

☐ assign more experienced people to work with younger individuals when small-group activities are used. This melds the real-world experience with the recentness of learning experience and offers an enhanced peer-group learning opportunity.

DIFFICULTIES IN TAKING TESTS AND/OR RECEIVING FEEDBACK

Not only do many adults dislike the idea of being tested; many have also forgotten how to prepare for and take tests. Finding the right place to study, taking the necessary time to study, being able to concentrate during the study and test periods, and similar skills may have to be relearned by your students. In addition, adults often fear feedback, and not all adults take feedback positively. Many adults have a natural tendency to argue and be defensive. In handling these situations, you should be prepared to respond to these concerns and to assume the roles of diplomat and negotiator.

Some of the fears associated with test taking can be overcome by

☐ explaining to the student the objectives of the test and the testing technique that will be used (e.g., short-answer, essay).

☐ providing students an opportunity before the test to practice taking the kind of test you will be using. This will virtually eliminate the potential shock of having to take a two-hour essay exam when all your students have been asked to do up to that time was to answer multiple-choice-question tests.

9

☐ clearly identifying for the student what knowledge and skill areas will be tested. Although you want to avoid telling them specifically what questions will be asked, you can give them hints in terms of what they will be expected to know, especially with a group of people who have been in the workplace for a number of years and who have not had to take tests within the last few years. As they gain experience in taking tests, you can reduce the number of hints.

☐ maintaining confidentiality of test scores. One of the biggest fears people have about testing is the fear of who will see the test results. If you keep the test scores strictly confidential and can convince the students of your desire to do this, you will have overcome this very large obstacle.

After grading tests and compiling the results, you have the important task of providing feedback—both positive and negative—to the student. Some tips for accomplishing this are the following:

☐ If someone has done very well on a test, congratulate her by writing notes such as "excellent" or "good job" on the test paper. This will continue to build her confidence.

☐ Return corrected tests promptly. In this way the information is still relatively fresh in the students' minds and helps relieve their anxiety over how they "did" on the test.

☐ Avoid just marking an answer as wrong; provide some feedback to the student about the correct answer. Occasionally, instructors do, of course, make mistakes. Providing the students with feedback about the right answer gives them the opportunity to challenge your thinking and to clear up any misconceptions that either you or the students may have.

☐ If someone's performance on tests is consistently below desired levels of competence, it may be worthwhile to spend some time with him to try to determine why. These discussions must be conducted in private in order to avoid embarrassing the student in front of his peers. You should try to determine the causes of the problems and be prepared to offer suggestions and/or opportunities for remediation so that his testing performance can be improved.

☐ Identify alternative reference sources that students can use to expand their information about a particular body of knowledge. Sometimes reading supplementary information by another author who takes a slightly different viewpoint on the subject is sufficient to eliminate misunderstandings.

BALANCE BETWEEN WORKLOAD, PERSONAL PRIORITIES, AND TRAINING

By contrast, adult learners are considered to be more mature than academic learners. The adult learner, being in the business world, is forced to divide his attention among family, business, financial, and social issues. A problem which arises in any one of these areas will significantly affect the individual's desire or ability to participate in training. This is not to say that the academic learner, whom we might describe as a full-time college student, is not also pressured by these same forces but the degree of affect that these have on him is not as significant. Therefore, as you design the training program, you need to recognize that these outside pressures exist and be flexible enough to work in concert with them.

USE OF REAL-WORLD DATA AND SITUATIONS

As we've mentioned before, adult learners respond most favorably to training situations that directly relate to their jobs. They also want the training to provide knowledge and skill development that they can apply directly and immediately to the tasks they are expected to perform on the job. This will require you, as the facilitator, to prepare for the training sessions by conducting research into the nature of the "real world." Some ways you can accomplish this are by talking with managers in the respective areas from which students will be coming, reading job descriptions to determine the roles and responsibilities of the individuals, and surveying the students themselves.

Then, as you structure the learning exercises, keep the results of this research in mind. If a class is composed of individuals whose

11

job involves data analysis, then an appropriate exercise might be for them to analyze a sample report that they normally use. If an individual's job is highly interactive, a case study that asks the student to explain how a situation might be handled could be appropriate. Where necessary, line up resource people who can facilitate key portions of the training session and who can be available to provide insight into how the concepts being discussed can have an impact in the real world. The use of subject-matter resources is discussed at length in chapter 8.

OPPORTUNITIES TO SHARE INFORMATION WITH OTHERS

For the majority of adults, peer-group learning is the most effective training technique. So as you design your training session, maximize the opportunities for individuals to share their ideas with the others in the group. From a facilitation standpoint, this virtually dictates that your presentations are short and that you emphasize a question-and-answer discussion technique, combined with small-group activities and hands-on practice.

Using small-group discussions has additional advantages. People are generally more willing to participate and receive feedback in a small, rather than a large, group setting. When doing problem-solving exercises, it is also easier to reach a consensus in a group of five to seven people than with a group of fifteen to twenty people. Small groups also tend to minimize the potentially adverse effect of individuals who take great pleasure in dominating discussions through loudness and intimidation. The use of small groups is discussed in greater detail in chapter 3.

CASE STUDIES

You can demonstrate the application of theory to actual circumstances through the use of case studies. Keep in mind, however, that not everyone likes to participate in them. Because case studies encourage people to take risks and to use their collective knowledge and skills to handle sample real-world problems, participation may be viewed as a threatening experience, especially when an individual is uneasy about demonstrating the level of ability she typically exhibits when performing her job.

When using case studies, design them so that they reflect real-world situations and thereby enable participants the opportunity to relate actual experiences and techniques to the sample problem. The design and use of case studies are discussed at greater length in the Instructional Techniques chapter.

THE IMPORTANCE OF INSTRUCTIONAL OBJECTIVES

- Help focus the program on the client's needs
- Help the manager and employee determine whether the program is appropriate for the employee
- Help you decide which instructional techniques are best to use
- Provide a measurement for learning
- Focus on end results

TIPS FOR CREATING INSTRUCTIONAL OBJECTIVES

- Make them easy to measure
- Use specific verbs like *list, write,* and *identify* rather than general verbs such as *understand*
- Tailor objectives to the desired level of competency

THE "MYSTERY"
OF INSTRUCTIONAL
OBJECTIVES

Now that you have had a chance to think about who you will be presenting your material to, you are ready to get down to the nuts and bolts of actually planning your training. The first step is to think through what you want to accomplish. What knowledge or skills do the participants need to have when they have completed your program? Establishing your objectives provides a solid foundation for the rest of the planning process.

The Importance of Instructional Objectives

Since the early 1970s, probably as a result of Robert Mager's book *Preparing Instructional Objectives,* professional trainers have been using a concept called *behavioral objectives.* Behavioral objectives identify what specific changes in a student's behavior are expected to occur during a training program.

Mager's concept reflected the basic idea that a training objective should be written in terms that are specific and easily measured. When used in conjunction with the design and development of a training program, your objectives can help you, the person or department responsible for the training's end result (called the *client*), and your students in the following ways.

1. By reaching an agreement with the client department at the outset of the design phase regarding the training program's objectives, there is an increased chance that your final program will correctly focus on and meet the client's desired training needs.

2. By reading the training program's objectives, both a manager and his or her subordinate can readily determine whether a specific program offers the content and depth of material necessary for the subordinate's desired professional growth.

3. By identifying the desired behavior change to be accomplished in a training program, you, as a facilitator, can better determine what instructional and evaluative techniques will be most appropriate during the session.

4. It provides both you and your students with a relatively accurate means for determining whether the desired learning objectives have been achieved.

5. It forces you, the client, students, and their managers to think about what knowledge and/or skills a student will come away from a program with rather than what knowledge they take into a program.

Tips for Creating Instructional Objectives

The key point to remember about instructional objectives is to make sure they can be measured easily and accurately. If you use phrases such as *to understand, to learn, to appreciate fully, to enjoy,* or *to grasp the significance of,* you will find your objectives difficult to measure. How do you really know when someone understands, has learned, or fully appreciates something? Instead, use terms such as the following:

to list	to solve
to describe	to construct
to explain	to compare
to write	to contrast
to identify	to differentiate

These phrases are open to fewer interpretations among different people and are more easily and accurately measured. Either the students can perform these functions or they cannot. In addition, ambiguous terms such as *to understand, learn, interpret,* and so forth mean different things to different people. Use of an objective such as "to understand how to use a computer" could mean being able to turn it on, log into the system, follow instructions displayed on the monitor, and turn it off. To others, it might mean having to write computer programs. Therefore, you need to break down these broad terms into smaller specific learning activities. You can do this by thinking through what exactly is involved in "understanding" something. By identifying each activity separately, you can determine how it can be clearly measured. Using the same computer example, some of the activities necessary to understanding how to operate a computer might better reflect a student's ability to

- [ ] locate the appropriate reference manual,
- [ ] turn on the system,
- [ ] log onto the system using the assigned code and password,
- [ ] describe the different screens available,
- [ ] demonstrate the ability to enter data correctly, and so forth.

By using this approach, there is a better chance that students will understand the computer's operation in the way the client had intended them to know it. Each step is specific in intent, and each can be easily measured to determine whether the students have grasped the concepts being taught.

The use of proper phrasing can also determine the depth of knowledge and/or skill that will be taught in a given training program. For example, if you want students to achieve a level of basic familiarity with a particular subject, you will probably use terms such as *to list* and *to identify* as behavioral objectives. If a more functional or higher competency level of knowledge and/or skill is expected from a program, it is likely that your objectives will also ask students *to describe, to explain,* and/or *to demonstrate* such knowledge and/or skills. If your students are expected to achieve a still higher, more proficient professional level of knowledge and/or skill, words such as *to analyze* or *to contrast* will likely be found among the objectives.

Since instructional objectives are indicative of the depth to which a subject is to be discussed, they also have a profound impact on the instructional and evaluative techniques used during the session. For example, to achieve an objective stating that students should be able "to list" something, such as the thirteen original colonies of the United States, requires you, as the instructor, merely to provide the information (e.g., in a presentation type of format) and ask the students to respond by correctly listing what they have been told.

Objectives stating that a student should be able "to describe" or "to explain" concepts such as the key components of a personal computer system require that you use a broader range of instructional techniques that not only provide information but also periodically test for comprehension. Appropriate techniques would include the question-and-answer, discussion, and the review approaches.

If students are asked "to demonstrate" knowledge such as how to operate a computer terminal, you should use a technique that illustrates how to conduct the operation properly and then provide opportunities for the students to apply what they have learned. Instructional techniques well suited for this include the demonstration/practice and case-study techniques.

For the higher knowledge and skill levels, where students are asked "to analyze" or "to contrast, " you need to integrate further all available instructional techniques, with a primary focus on obtaining feedback from the students in order to measure relative comprehension and creativity in approaching the various problems. One excellent means for accomplishing this goal is the use of comprehensive case studies that will encourage your students to look at issues from several different perspectives (e.g., Analyze the impact of implementing a new computer system in the XYZ Company which will have the ability to ...).

Chapter 4 contains more detail about each of these different instructional techniques.

WHAT TO CONSIDER WHEN DESIGNING
A PROGRAM

- What the audience knows
- How much time is available for training
- How complex the material is
- Whether special equipment will be available
- When the training will be used on the job

TIPS FOR PROGRAM DESIGN

- Think in terms of an average student
- Be creative
- Draw upon the experiences of your students

DESIGNING THE
TRAINING PROGRAM

In designing your program, selecting the most appropriate instructional technique for communicating the subject material could well mean the difference between a successful and an unsuccessful training effort. As a facilitator, you are responsible for having a thorough knowledge of the information to be discussed and being comfortable with a variety of different instructional techniques. Both of these elements are necessary in order for you to anticipate reasonably how the information can be communicated most effectively.

The first step in selecting an instructional technique is to refer to the program's objectives. As mentioned in the earlier chapter, if your desired learning outcomes focus on the students' ability to identify, define, list, or describe informational elements, the instructional techniques you use can be relatively simple and straightforward. On the other hand, if your objectives require the student to analyze, compare, contrast, and use similar higher-level cognitive skills, the instructional techniques you use will be more complex.

Factors Affecting Program Design

Once you have established a sense of the overall desired learning level, there are other factors you need to consider when designing and developing your training program. These factors would include, but are not limited to the

- ☐ knowledge and skill level of the audience;
- ☐ time available for training;
- ☐ complexity of the material being discussed;
- ☐ dependency upon, and availability of, special equipment (e.g., computer terminals);
- ☐ implementation timing.

Let's take a look at each of these factors individually.

KNOWLEDGE AND SKILL LEVEL OF THE AUDIENCE

The training task becomes more simplified if you are aware of people in the audience who may already have a familiarity with the concepts being discussed. Such people enable you to use the peer-group learning concept and, through the techniques of asking questions or conducting demonstrations, to bring out the knowledge and skill levels of these individuals and shift the burden of training temporarily to someone else. But obviously, if the information is totally new, it is unlikely that anyone in the audience will be able to assist in the training by providing background experience. Thus, the learning procedure you use will have to follow a more step-by-step process and will require more time to complete.

You can obtain information about the background and experience levels of the participants by several means. First, by knowing what functions members of the audience currently perform, you can use your intuition about how new the subject is to your audience. For example, you can probably anticipate that a training session on performance-evaluation techniques for a group of new supervisors is likely to have one or more persons in attendance who have some experience with the material being discussed. On the other hand, in introducing a new computer system, you run a high risk of finding very few, if any, people in the audience who have a depth of knowledge or skill in the new process.

You can also determine information through discussions with the managers and/or supervisors of the participants, through pre-session questionnaires, or by direct contact with the individuals themselves.

TIME AVAILABLE FOR TRAINING

Given enough time, anybody could be trained to do anything. Unfortunately, this luxury of unlimited training time does not exist in the business community. In fact, needing to have the training completed yesterday—on the students' own time—is more often the case.

Although most training is traditionally accomplished in full-day segments, this may not always be appropriate. Factors that could have an impact on the training time available to you could include

☐ *time of the year.* Summer vacations and major holiday periods tend to reduce overall staff levels and could mean that a functional unit would be left unattended if the available person in the office were attending a training program.

☐ *financial closings.* Within many businesses, accounting activities are heaviest during the last week in the month, quarter, and/or year. Dealing with an organization's financial health has always taken precedence over involvement in training; therefore, it would be impractical to try to have someone who is involved in these financial activities participate in a training program during these periods.

☐ *work coverage.* Similar to the concerns about time of year, it would be impractical to suggest that an entire work unit be involved in a training session, because no one would be available to answer telephones, respond to management information requests, and handle "rush" items.

☐ *workload.* The volume of work activity in a unit may make it necessary for you to be creative in planning how a training program is to be conducted. Although the training session may be viewed as important, you may have to work around the ongoing concerns an individual and/or manager might have about how attendance at the session might affect the individual's ability to handle his or her workload. One possible alternative could be a shared-time approach in which a one-hour training program is conducted partly on personal time and partly during normal work hours. Some training programs may only be one-shot deals where the shared-time concept might be appropriate. In other cases, a more lengthy training program could be set up using this same approach where the class meets a couple of times during the week or perhaps on the same day for several consecutive weeks. Whatever the case, the shared-time approach has been used effectively as a training alternative. It gives the impression to both management and the students that training is the responsibility of both parties and that some compromises may be necessary in order for training to be successfully implemented.

COMPLEXITY OF THE MATERIAL BEING DISCUSSED

Regardless of whether technical resources are available or whether individual audience members are already somewhat knowledgeable about the concepts being discussed, the fact remains that the more complex the material, the slower the pace of learning involved.

Complex training programs are essentially those that require the learner to acquire new skills, such as those needed when a new computer system is installed, or that require the integration of facts, concepts, and processes to produce results that are not readily apparent. An example of the latter might be the requirement for a learner to develop a set of action-plan recommendations based on financial trend data, organizational staffing formulas, business-plan growth projections, and planned economic growth of a community. A good measure of a program's complexity is the degree to which the students have been exposed to this information in the past.

Remember, what may be basic to you (because of your level of training or experience) may be totally foreign to your students. Therefore, the more complex the program, from the learner's standpoint, the more you need to build into the program opportunities to practice the new skills and receive constructive feedback. This is necessary if you want to monitor the students' progress during the program, identify whether the desired learning is being achieved, and provide any necessary remedial work in a timely fashion. When you have a complex training program, it may also be necessary to have subject-matter resources available to answer detailed technical questions that may arise. Techniques for obtaining the support of these subject-matter resources is covered in chapter 8.

DEPENDENCY UPON AND AVAILABILITY
OF SPECIAL EQUIPMENT

The best example of special equipment that may be needed for a training session would be computer terminals, or CRTs. If the training includes the development of an individual's ability to use computer systems effectively through a CRT, a sufficient number of terminals need to be available. Most likely, these units would need to be separate from the production terminals, otherwise their use might adversely affect unit productivity. However, this would also require that such a satellite facility have its terminals wired into the central computer system. This can be a relatively expensive and difficult task.

Another concern is the ratio of the number of students to terminals. A rule of thumb is to have no more than three students on a single terminal. In such a situation, one person practices keyboarding, another researches to determine input values, and the third performs a quality-control function. Throughout the training, participants rotate among these three positions.

If too few terminals are available, students can acquire the desired skills in other ways. Off-hour terminal use and paper-and-pencil practice exercises are two possible alternatives.

IMPLEMENTATION TIMING

As the facilitator, you need to know how soon after the training program the skills are expected to be used. If detailed training is provided on a system that will not be available and operational until three to six months after the session, the trainees will forget much of the information unless you support it with written material that can be used as reference when the system finally comes on-line. In this scenario it would also be appropriate to consider offering a refresher course just prior to system implementation, if the time and budget allow.

Guidelines for Program Design

As you begin to design your course and think about how you will present the material, it will help to keep the following guidelines in mind.

CONSIDER YOURSELF TO BE YOUR OWN AVERAGE STUDENT

When you are designing a training program, it is virtually impossible to outguess your students continually. A good yardstick, however, is yourself and how you feel you would like to learn. If you, as the instructor, consider yourself to be an average student in your own class, then you will have a better idea of how well a technique and/or exercise will be received.

By thinking in terms of the average student, you are more likely to focus the design of the program on the majority of students. If you gear the program to the over- or underachievers in the group, there is a higher likelihood that others will lose interest in the session because the program will be moving either too fast or too slow. Also, by considering yourself as your own average student, you can better judge whether your plans for approaching a subject or an exercise that you plan to use will be effective. If you do not feel comfortable with it, then the chance is that your students will not like it either.

Since individuals learn at different rates, using this approach helps establish an approximate time it will take to learn the material. If you can anticipate how complex the material will be to learn and how much reinforcement will be needed to ensure understanding, then you will have a better idea of how long it will take to complete the training successfully.

BE WILLING TO TRY CREATIVE APPROACHES

When it comes to being creative, you can become your own worst enemy. Your lack of desire to experiment with new techniques or new approaches to common problems is the only thing that stands in your way of being creative during a training session.

To grow as a skilled facilitator, you need to go beyond the normal bounds of training. When you find yourself in a training situation, experiment with things you would not normally do and see how well they work. If they are successful, add them to your "bag of tricks" for use during subsequent sessions. If these new approaches are not successful, analyze why not, make changes, and try again, if appropriate. Again, use yourself as an average student and ask yourself what you might consider to be a dynamic presentation of this material. If you feel a creative technique will work, then others in the group will probably agree.

FIND OUT WHAT STUDENTS KNOW

Because the peer-group learning concept is so important to the way adults learn, it is important that you, as a facilitator, maximize the involvement of your students. All too often, an instructor spends the majority of time during a training session telling his or her students what they need to know about a given subject. Little, if any, time is spent asking the students what they know, how they feel, and/or how they might handle given situations.

If you take this approach with your students, you will merely prove that you know the material. You will obtain, however, little feedback on whether the information is properly received, translated and/or can be applied by the students. In essence, you will have virtually no idea how much the students know about the subject being presented. Therefore, the more you can draw upon the experiences of your students, the greater the amount of peer-group learning that takes place. Other advantages in this approach are that it makes it easier for you to communicate the information to your students and it provides you with a means for expanding your own knowledge of the material by hearing the collective experiences and comments of others.

INSTRUCTIONAL TECHNIQUES

- Presentation
- Question-and-answer discussion
- Small-group discussion
- Demonstration/practice
- Case study
- Review

INSTRUCTIONAL
TECHNIQUES

To be a good facilitator, you need to strive to maximize the results of your training session. In the adult learning environment, this can be done through a variety of instructional techniques which, if used properly, can achieve a positive atmosphere within which peer-group learning can take place. For most training sessions it is rare that only one instructional technique will be appropriate. Perhaps the only time this might be the case is during a session that lasts a maximum of fifteen minutes. Thus, your responsibility is to know what techniques are available and how to use them effectively, especially in combination with one or more other techniques.

This chapter describes some of the more traditional instructional techniques that are available. With some careful planning, you can tailor each technique to provide sufficient opportunities for your participants to tell what they know and/or demonstrate their skills for a given subject. The resulting benefits of successful implementation are twofold: (1) it will provide an atmosphere of openness within which participants will be willing to share their thoughts and ideas, and (2) it will provide you with ongoing opportunities for feedback in order to measure how effectively the learning is taking place.

The discussion of each technique will give you some idea of its advantages and disadvantages, a general description of how it can be implemented, common pitfalls that should be avoided, and examples of when and how it can be used. Remember, the key to becoming an effective instructor is your willingness to experiment with new techniques, to put yourself in the place of your students in order to anticipate how a desired instructional approach will be received, to practice each technique until it becomes second nature, and to learn from and build upon your successes and mistakes.

Presentation Technique

Key points to remember:

☐ Be sure you know what learning objectives you want to achieve

☐ Integrate with other instructional techniques to balance the training session

☐ Support with effective visual aids

☐ Use to provide a strong opening and closing to the training session

GENERAL DESCRIPTION

The basic objective of many training programs is to communicate information. This can be done through either a lecture or a presentation. With a lecture, students are given almost no opportunity for feedback. Its purpose is to communicate information in a short period of time to a large heterogeneous audience. A lecture, however, does not have to be held in a stuffy, crowded classroom. Think about the last time you flew on a commercial airliner. The introduction that the flight attendants make concerning the aircraft's safety features is a lecture because they do not ask for feedback and are communicating information to a varied audience (i.e., people of different ages and nationalities, with varied flying experience, etc.) in a short period of time.

Presentations, although similar to lectures, tend to be less formal. In fact, this technique is frequently referred to as a lecturette. When using this technique, a discussion leader provides more frequent opportunities for feedback by asking questions throughout the presentation. The aircraft-safety-introduction example would become a presentation if the flight attendant in the middle of her talk asks a question such as, "Who can demonstrate the proper use of the oxygen mask; perhaps the person in seat 15C?"

Because the presentation technique is a less formal means for communicating information and because it is generally used with other instructional techniques, it has become a very popular technique used with training programs. Unfortunately, it is also one of the most abused techniques. Let's now look at what makes this technique effective.

ADVANTAGES AND DISADVANTAGES

Advantages

1. Facilitates communication of information in a short period of time. As frequently happens, training time may become

limited, but the requirement that information still be communicated without delay remains. In such circumstances the presentation technique provides the best use of the time available, because its primary purpose is to transmit information without allowing much discussion.

2. Offers effective means for providing new information and/ or for clarifying existing information. Interactive techniques such as question-and-answer discussion or small-group activities are inappropriate when new information is being discussed. Therefore, as the facilitator, you must build this level of knowledge and/or skills so that more interactive techniques can be used. The same holds true where it is important to clarify information so that a common and correct level of understanding exists about a given subject.

3. Is useful for communicating transitional and supporting information. To be a good facilitator, you should look at a training session as an exercise in time management. You must then decide what information is important and what is "filler." Therefore, only the material that directly relates to the achievement of the session's objectives requires the group's involvement. Material used to make transitions from subject A to subject B or to provide supporting information for a point can be communicated more effectively through a brief presentation than through a more time-consuming interactive exercise.

4. Provides excellent means for setting the stage for the session by providing program/discussion parameters, communicating the "givens," and so forth. To be effective, you need to recognize the value not only of making the first five minutes interesting but also of laying the necessary groundwork and parameters for the training session. You can use the presentation technique effectively to communicate the program's objectives and also to make it very clear to the participants what subjects are open and closed for discussion. This provides your students with a roadmap of what to expect during the session and decreases the chance of their focusing on a subject that is beyond the bounds of the group.

5. Provides a means for making an easy transition to other techniques. The presentation technique can easily be used with other, more interactive techniques. For example, a presentation can be used to introduce a small-group exercise, summarize its results, make a transition to the next subject, introduce the next exercise, and so forth.

6. Is useful for communicating to large audiences. Although most training sessions will involve small groups of eight people or less, there may be times when a larger group is involved or when there is no opportunity to subdivide the large group into smaller groups. In such situations a presentation of the information is the only good instructional alternative. The task then becomes finding ways to be creative and make the presentation interesting.

7. Is good for covering underlying concepts, principles, and systems. Cold, hard facts are rarely exciting but often very important to discuss and usually are necessary for building the foundation upon which further discussions and exercises can be based. In some cases these facts may be new information or a clarification or reinforcement of existing information and, as stated earlier, can best be communicated in a presentation rather than through a more interactive technique.

Disadvantages

1. Places the burden of promoting learning fully on you, the instructor, unless the technique is integrated with other techniques. A common problem with presentations is that you will need to use all your creative powers in order to make the subject interesting. Creativity, however, lasts for only short periods of time. An instructor who uses a presentation as his or her primary means of communicating information therefore constantly faces the challenge of making the subject interesting to the student and thereby assumes the majority of the burden for how well a subject is being learned.

2. Establishes a "tell me" mind-set with the students. Students sense very quickly how much they are going to have to

work during a training session. If the first fifteen minutes of a program are nothing but presentation, students will tend to lapse into a listening rather than a participatory mode. The longer the presentation continues, the less the students will be willing to participate and contribute. The burden of learning therefore builds upon the instructor.

3. Offers limited opportunities for feedback. Unless a presentation is formally integrated with more interactive techniques, it will be very difficult for you to receive feedback on how well the information is coming across and whether the students are receiving and translating it properly. Without a plan for how feedback will be acquired, you can only hope that students will ask questions or that you will be able to recognize positive nonverbal cues.

4. Becomes a crutch for instructors who do not really know the material thoroughly. As an instructor, you do not have to be an expert in the material being discussed, but you should have a strong enough background in the subject's principles and concepts to sustain a positive learning experience for your students. As frequently happens, however, instructors use the presentation technique to communicate all they know about the subject and do not provide opportunities for "threatening" questions to be asked. Such instructors feel the basic idea is to get through the material as quickly as possible and not be concerned about how well the material has been communicated.

5. Requires that information be supplemented by visual aids. Studies have shown that information received through the sense of hearing has a very short retention span. On the other hand, information obtained through the visual senses is retained much longer. Therefore, because a presentation is geared to the auditory senses, its retention can only be improved by using visual aids such as flipcharts, handouts, or CRTs to support what is being discussed. Some of these visual aids are discussed in chapter 5.

6. Can lead to students' saturation with information. Using a presentation technique to communicate principles, concepts, and similar factual information may produce "infor-

mation overload" unless the presentation is moderated with opportunities to practice and apply what has been learned. Remember, the adult learner wants to be able to apply the information on the job as soon as possible and therefore concentrates throughout the session on how this can be done.

7. Can lead to boredom, especially if the information is highly technical and generic. Unless you seek to make the factual information interesting and can devise creative means for communicating it, the participants may become bored. Your task then becomes one of anticipating how much of this information can be communicated effectively during the session and designing the training program accordingly.

PITFALLS TO AVOID

When designing and building a training program in which you will use the presentation technique to a large extent, consider these potential pitfalls:

1. Having a poor lesson plan. An effective lesson plan will build on the advantages of the presentation technique and minimize the inherent disadvantages. Chapter 6 discusses lesson plans in detail.

2. Relying too heavily on the technique. Although the technique is good for communicating important information, too much of a good thing can be a problem. Try to balance a presentation with other techniques that you reasonably expect will be effective in addressing the subject material.

3. Allowing students to develop an improper or unintended mind-set. If you want the session to be interactive, then this mind-set has to be established early and maintained throughout the session. Too much presentation at the beginning of a training session will condition your students to listen rather than participate.

4. Having poor presentation and/or facilitation skills. Because the burden for communicating the information falls upon you, the instructor, it is imperative that you have effective

presentation skills. Problems with distracting mannerisms, tone of voice, rate of speech, and improper use of various instructional and visual aids can seriously affect how well the information is communicated. More discussion of these presentation skills appears in chapter 7.

5. Making an insufficient allowance for feedback. Although you may be having a good time telling students the information, your job is not complete unless some means have been provided to determine how well the information has been received and whether it can be applied effectively. Not everyone has a strong ability to "read" the audience to determine their reactions. And even if one has the ability, are the signals being received accurate? The only sure way to know is for you to give students opportunities to ask questions or participate in exercises so you will know if the information you are giving is being understood.

KEYS TO EFFECTIVE IMPLEMENTATION

On the basis of the advantages and disadvantages and the potential pitfalls just described, some criteria for effective implementation of the presentation technique are the following:

1. *Know which of the program's objectives are to be wholly or partially achieved by the presentation.* If there are none, then use the presentation only to introduce your material and make transitions. Remember, to be an effective facilitator, you must use your time and effort wisely.

2. *Integrate the presentation with other interactive techniques early in the program.* This conditions the audience not only to listen but to be prepared to respond to questions and to offer their thoughts, opinions, and ideas.

3. *Develop good supporting visual aids.* The longer the presentation, the more visual aids that will be needed to support it. Chapter 5 deals with how to develop visual aids effectively.

4. *Have a strong opening and closing to the session.* Although the opening five minutes of a session are critical for es-

tablishing the climate of the training session, the closing is equally important because this will be the last thing that people will remember about the session. Be very clear about any homework requirements (e.g., exercises to be completed, pages to be read), the schedule for next session, and so forth. Be sure the entire session is a positive experience from start to finish.

5. Be aware of gestures, posture, tone of voice, and other presentation skills. When doing a presentation, you are in the spotlight; therefore, the longer the presentation, the longer you are on center stage. If necessary, practice your presentation skills in front of a mirror and use a cassette recorder so you can hear how well you come across. Do you like what you see and hear? If not, change it, because the chances are that others will not like it either.

EXAMPLES FOR IMPLEMENTATION

The following is one illustration of how a presentation can be used during a training session and integrated with other techniques to maximize interaction, place some of the burden of learning on the students, and provide opportunities for feedback.

This example assumes that a group of six people are being trained in the use of a new computer system, with the training to last two hours each day for one week. CRTs are available for the students to practice on, and workbooks have been provided that enable the students to take notes as the session progresses. This might be a typical first-day session.

Type of Material Being Discussed	Technique Used	Approximate Time
Introduction to the session by department head or chief instructor	Presentation	10 min.
Concerns students have about new system	Small groups	30 min.
Feedback on students' concerns (communicated by spokesperson for the group)	Presentation	20 min.

Type of Material Being Discussed	Technique Used	Approximate Time
New system's concepts and principles (overview)	Presentation	30 min.
Perceived impact that these changes will have on the company and the job responsibilities of each student	Question-and-answer discussion or small-group discussion	15 min.
Feedback on group's perceptions	Presentation	10 min.
Summary of day 1 and assignments for day 2	Review/presentation	5 min.

This example illustrates how the presentation technique can be used in concert with other techniques and how a group can be acclimated quickly to working rather than listening. These types of exercises are useful for determining what concerns the students may have about the new system and the extent to which they may view the system as a threat to their present jobs. Once the students have aired their concerns, you can better anticipate how they will perceive information and adjust your future presentations and exercises accordingly.

Question-and-Answer Discussion Technique

Key points to remember:

☐ Know what learning objectives you are trying to accomplish

☐ Have a clear understanding of the total training situation

☐ Know the types of questions to ask and when to use them

☐ Manage the training time effectively

GENERAL DESCRIPTION

The question-and-answer discussion technique involves the art of seeking information and stimulating thinking to achieve a given objective. This technique is used to span the full range of human reasoning, from the level of recalling facts to making discrete judgments on unique problems.

The reason for using questions as an instructional technique is to maximize the amount of interaction that takes place in the class. The greater the extent to which individuals feel they participated in and contributed to a discussion, the greater the likelihood that these individuals will feel the session was valuable and the time well spent. In using this technique, there are basically two kinds of questions: open-ended and closed-ended. An open-ended question is one that allows the respondent to answer and elaborate in any manner he or she feels is necessary. Such questions usually begin with words or phrases such as *what are, where did, why are, how can, tell me,* and so forth. Closed-ended questions limit the response to a specific type of answer such as yes or no.

ADVANTAGES AND DISADVANTAGES

Advantages

1. Effectively transfers the burden of learning to the student. By asking questions, you, as the facilitator, take the burden of providing all the answers and shift some of this responsibility onto the shoulders of the students. Of course, this does not decrease the need for you to know the material; you cannot try to "fake it" by asking questions and hoping that the students know the answer.

2. Increases the involvement of students in the learning process. As was mentioned in the section on the presentation technique, a common problem to be avoided was having students fall into a listening rather than a participatory frame of mind. Asking questions gets the learners involved and establishes an atmosphere conducive to the exchange of thoughts and ideas.

3. Provides both the adult learner and you, the instructor, with immediate feedback. Through questions you can determine whether the information has been received and translated correctly. Thus, both you and your students know almost immediately how effectively a concept has been communicated and understood, whether any misunderstandings exist, and what corrective action may be necessary to address any problems.

4. Is useful for guiding students to higher levels of inquiry. Questions help you probe an issue in more depth, beyond what might be considered merely an appropriate response. This helps you pinpoint the extent of the learner's capacity to apply the concepts being discussed and at the same time enables the learner to think beyond the normal bounds about how a problem can be analyzed.

5. Helps trigger stimuli. The use of questions can help you identify what makes a student "tick." The answers to questions such as "How do you feel about . . . ?" can reveal many underlying attitudes and opinions that a student may bring into the classroom environment. It can also give you valuable clues about how best to help your students learn and what their motivations are for learning.

Disadvantages

1. Can lead to too much reliance on questions. Although the use of questions is an effective strategy for maximizing group involvement, you can have too much of a good thing. Asking and answering questions takes time, and if time is a limited commodity—as it usually is—you should carefully weigh the technique of asking questions against what program objectives need to be achieved.

2. Is potentially ineffective if the audience is either not prepared or uninformed. The use of the question-and-answer discussion technique must assume that the people in the audience are somewhat able to respond positively to the questions asked. If during a session you discover that the students do not have the prerequisite knowledge or skill level, and you begin to realize that the question-and-answer

technique will be ineffective, you will need to immediately change facilitation tactics in order to accomplish the desired objectives.

3. Can encourage a dominant few in the class to answer questions. It is not unusual for a facilitator to be in a situation where one or more individuals in the audience try to control the discussion. Their motivation might be to try to impress others or exert their status among the group, and having the opportunity to answer questions provides them the ideal stage upon which to voice their ideas and opinions. Should this occur, you will need to bring them under control so the creative learning environment is not destroyed.

PITFALLS TO AVOID

The question-and-answer discussion technique is a very effective instructional tool for maximizing the involvement of students in the classroom. Like any other technique, though, it is only effective if used properly. This can be accomplished partly by avoiding the following pitfalls:

1. Using the technique to impart knowledge rather than to stimulate and direct learning inquiry. Plan questions carefully to stimulate the thinking of the group and to achieve an atmosphere in which the students can learn from their peers. Questions are not used to their fullest potential if they are structured only to retrieve facts and not to test how well these facts are understood and where they can be applied.

2. Having the discussion controlled by a dominant few. This is one of the surest ways to frustrate a class. With few exceptions, people do not come into a training program wanting the discussion controlled by the loudest or highest-ranking individuals in the audience. Instead, they are there to learn things that will help them on their jobs and to have an opportunity to exchange ideas with others in a relatively noncritical, safe environment. As the facilitator, you must tactfully control these dominant individuals by, perhaps,

intentionally avoiding them and directing questions to others; asking class members to elaborate on these individuals' comments (especially if you suspect that their comments are incorrect or their ideas and opinions are not shared by the majority of students); or, if the situation is critical, taking them aside and making them aware of what effect their attempt at control is having on the rest of the class.

3. Establishing a one-on-one rapport with a student at the expense of the others in the class. It is frequently very frustrating to a class to have an instructor set up a one-on-one dialogue with a student concerning a particular issue that may have relevance to only a few students. When this occurs, the instructor has effectively ignored the remainder of the class and provided them opportunities to escape mentally from the learning environment. Using a strategy of redirecting the question to others in the class is one way of resolving this potential problem.

KEYS TO EFFECTIVE IMPLEMENTATION

Your key to success in using the question-and-answer discussion technique is for you to plan carefully how the questions can be best integrated into the curriculum. To accomplish this, you need to do the following:

1. *Understanding the program's objectives.* Before any instructional planning can be accomplished effectively, you must clearly understand what is to be accomplished during the training program. As was stated earlier, the instructional task varies in complexity if the program's objectives are merely for the students to define and explain facts or situations rather than to have the students analyze, compare, and so forth, because the latter requires more instructional effort and skill.

2. *Analyze the learning situation.* To be effective, you should also look at all the other elements in the training scenario. This would include the experience level of the audience; the need for and availability of subject-matter resources

(e.g., for handling any highly technical questions); the time available for training; the nature of the material being presented (e.g., new versus revised); and the quality and availability of supporting information such as texts, job aids, and similar information that can be used for reinforcement of the learning. The results of analyzing each of these elements will help you determine what questions to ask, when to ask them, and what results to expect from the discussions.

3. *Know what types of questions can be asked and being able to anticipate when each can be used most effectively.* This would include knowing when to use open-ended questions, which allow students to elaborate on the points being discussed, or closed-ended questions, which tend to direct the students' answers more toward a desired response.

4. *Be able to understand and apply the principles of effective time management.* You should be able to anticipate how long a question-and-answer discussion segment will last and determine whether sufficient time is available to include this as a technique within the training program. Failure to adhere to time-management concepts can have detrimental effects on a training program. For example, if people are learning to operate a new computer system, and an arrangement has been made to use on-line terminals for practice purposes from 10:00 to 11:00 A.M., the work-unit manager is expecting you to have your people there on time. If you inappropriately decide to use a question-and-answer technique and are not able to complete the desired material until 10:35 A.M., you will have succeeded in effectively reducing the students' important hands-on time by more than 50 percent.

Once you are positive that a question-and-answer discussion technique is appropriate for achieving the desired objectives and that it can be completed within the given time frame, you should then consider what questioning strategies are most effective. Remember, the central reason for using this technique is to maximize the interaction that will take place within the classroom.

Some effective questioning strategies are to do the following.

1. *Use leading questions.* Leading questions are a type of closed-ended question through which you can direct an individual to respond in a desired manner. Leading questions can only be answered by a yes or no response and/or represent questions where the answer is contained in the question (i.e., a question that does not allow explanation). Such questions are often used as a means of introducing a new topic or making a transition from one topic to another. For example, during a computer-literacy program, you may want to ask, "Has anyone ever heard of the term *software* before?" because someone probably will be able to say yes to this question and, as a result, provide a base upon which you can move to the subject of software.

2. *Ask the question first and then direct it to an individual.* Most people do just the opposite. By asking, "Mary, what is the answer to question 4?" you let everyone off the hook in thinking about the answer to the question (except Mary, of course). However, by asking the question first and then directing it to Mary, you force everyone to consider the question (especially if you pause briefly before identifying Mary as the lucky individual), thereby further maximizing everyone's involvement in the learning process.

3. *Redirect questions whenever possible (and appropriate).* If a student asks a question that you feel can be answered by someone else in the class, you can further maximize learner involvement by asking others in the class to answer the question. This strategy also serves to encourage class members to learn from each other, thereby expanding the peer-group learning concept. You need to exercise restraint, however, and not overuse this strategy.

4. *Be willing to say "I don't know."* Despite your confidence in a classroom, there will be times when you are unable to answer a question. Students are generally more savvy about what they are being taught than we, as instructors, would like to believe; they can be fooled just so many times before realizing you do not really know much about the material

being presented. The result is a serious loss of credibility which may take a long time to recover. Of course, if you do indicate that you do not know the information, you must quickly seek the answer and communicate it to the group. In such cases you have the option of bearing this research burden yourself or assigning the "project" to one or more students. The answer to the problem can then be presented at the next class session.

EXAMPLES FOR IMPLEMENTATION

For the purpose of illustration, let's use a situation in which the focus of the training class is to introduce a new computer to an audience that is relatively inexperienced in using computer hardware or software. A possible two-hour training session that would accomplish the objective of providing the students with a basic level of knowledge about computer hardware and software might be structured as follows:

Training Activity to Be Conducted	Technique Used	Time Involved
Introduction of session's objectives	Presentation	10 min.
Question: "How many people have used a computer before?"	Closed-ended question	1 min.
Question (to a person who responded positively): "What have you liked about it?"	Open-ended question	3 min.
Question (to another person who responded positively): "What concerns do you have about using computers?"	Open-ended question	5 min.
Discussion of uses and advantages/disadvantages of computers	Presentation	20 min.
Question: "What do you see as the greatest advantages computers can have for your job, Sue?"	Open-ended question	5 min.
Question: "Can you see other advantages beyond what Sue has said, Jane?"	Open-ended question	5 min.

Training Activity to Be Conducted	Technique Used	Time Involved
Question: "What do I mean when I say *computer hardware*, Mike?"	Transition (open-ended) question	2 min.
Discussion of computer hardware	Presentation	20 min.
Question: "What kind of computer hardware do you have in your unit, Bill?"	Closed-ended question	2 min.
Question: "What do I mean when I say *computer software*, Kathy?"	Transition (open-ended) question	5 min.
Discussion of computer software	Presentation	20 min.
Question: "Consider your work area; what kinds of tasks would you like to have done by a computer, George?"	Open-ended question	5 min.
Question: "Do you have any others, Sam?"	Open-ended question	3 min.
Question: "Does anyone have any others to add to this list?"	Open-ended question	3 min.
Discussion of the programming concept	Presentation	6 min.
Summary of session, assignment for next session	Review/presentation	5 min.

This sample training session illustrates how questions can be used to begin a discussion, shift points, and stimulate participation. The first set of questions seeks to identify whether any potential resources are in the audience. Note that the first question—"How many people have used a computer before?"—is phrased as an open-ended question. However, because it will receive only a limited answer, it is more like a closed-ended question that serves as a transition for students to the new subject matter. Assuming that Mike and Jane had indicated some familiarity with computers, they could then each be the target of the later leading questions. The more general questions relating to what hardware is used in the unit and the requests for additional comments are examples of how the question-and-answer technique can be used to bring others into the discussion in a nonthreatening manner, thereby signaling to others that it is okay to participate.

48

Small-Group Discussion Technique

Key points to remember:

☐ Listen attentively

☐ Remain impartial

☐ Introduce and conclude the technique properly

☐ Make sure each group has a cross-section of knowledge and experience

☐ Control off-track discussions

☐ Circulate among the work groups

☐ Guide rather than influence

☐ Provide positive reinforcement

☐ Arrange group seating to maximize interaction

☐ Change group assignments as appropriate

GENERAL DESCRIPTION

Small groups consist of between two and eight people. Once a group expands beyond this number, the dynamics of group interaction take on more of the characteristics of a large group, especially regarding the degree to which individuals are willing to contribute ideas, discuss issues, and reach consensus agreements. The most effective peer-group learning takes place in a small-group setting; therefore, whenever possible, you should try to structure training exercises into this learning format.

ADVANTAGES AND DISADVANTAGES

Advantages

1. Facilitates communication more than a large-group setting does. The small group gives individuals more of a feeling of being an integral part of the group. As a result, they are more willing to introduce, discuss, and critique ideas than if

more people were involved. In general, a small-group environment provides individuals with a greater feeling that their contributions will be considered important and that others will want to listen to their ideas.

2. Stimulates peer-group learning. Because individuals are more willing to exchange their thoughts, opinions, and experiences in a small-group setting, they have a better opportunity to learn from each other.

3. Makes it easier for people to reach a consensus. The smaller the group, the easier it is to reach an agreement on conclusions and/or actions to be taken.

4. Fosters a closer working relationship among team members. The smaller the group, the less time it takes to get to know other members of the group. Because one of the major barriers to effective interpersonal relations is the fact that one individual might not be comfortable in working with someone else, a small group can provide the proper setting to overcome this barrier and therefore stimulate a sense of cooperation among members.

5. Enables you, as an instructor, to use other techniques such as case studies. For maximum benefit, case studies take time to implement and discuss; however, the smaller the group, the fewer the number of conclusions or solutions that need to be discussed, and therefore the better the management of the training time. A later section in this chapter provides more information on the case-study technique.

Disadvantages

1. Makes it easy for participants to get into off-track discussions. Because small groups tend to be more informal, their discussions also tend to include various examples and personal experiences, not all of which may be relevant to the subject being discussed. Therefore, it is important that you periodically listen to what the small-group participants are discussing and bring them back on track as quickly as possible if they have strayed from the desired path.

2. Is very time consuming (requires proper introduction, implementation, and summary). When the small-group technique is used as part of a large-group training session, you should let everyone know what activity is to take place, what objectives are to be accomplished, and how much time is available to accomplish the task. Time must then be allowed for the large group to divide into the desired small-group segments, conduct the activity, and reassemble into the large-group format. Using a case study as an example, this process could take thirty minutes or more to complete.

3. Increases potential for interpersonal conflicts. Small groups provide an excellent opportunity for group members to get to know each other and to exchange thoughts and ideas more informally. As a result, use of the small-group technique also increases the possibility that disagreements might arise among various work-group members. Therefore, it is important for you to anticipate sources of these problems (e.g., not putting into the same group two people who you know do not work well together); to minimize the effect on the rest of the audience of such problems, should they arise; and to assure that such interpersonal conflicts do not leave the confines of the training session.

4. Requires careful structuring of the composition of the group. In addition to facing the need to separate potential adversaries from each other, you also should be sure that the group's composition represents the right cross-section of talent necessary to solve the given problem. It may be necessary to determine ahead of time what this proper group composition should be and to assign the participants to these groups accordingly.

PITFALLS TO AVOID

When implementing a small-group technique, you should be careful to avoid the following:

1. Taking sides on an issue rather than encouraging further discussion. An instructor often agrees with the arguments

51

being presented by one group rather than those of another group. However, by becoming too involved in the discussion and/or openly taking sides with one group, you lose the capability of being able to maximize the discussion of all sides of the issue. Because many people view you, the instructor, as being an authority on the subject, you run the risk of alienating a segment, or perhaps even a majority, of the audience.

2. Allowing off-track discussions. A small-group discussion can stimulate a highly interactive exchange of thoughts and ideas among participants. In such an environment it is not unusual to have more than one discussion going on simultaneously or to have the major discussion bog down in a mire of irrelevant arguments and examples. If allowed to go unchecked, such occurrences will seriously hamper attainment of the session's objectives. This could ultimately affect the participants' overall perceptions of your skill as a discussion leader and facilitator.

3. Allowing interpersonal conflicts to leave the room. In order to maintain a healthy on-the-job working climate, you must confine to the classroom any interpersonal conflicts that may arise. Allowing these differences to filter into the workplace can cause long-lasting credibility problems for both you and the parties involved.

KEYS TO EFFECTIVE IMPLEMENTATION

Use of the small-group technique can produce some of the most effective interactive training sessions, because this technique provides ample opportunity for participants to discuss information and to learn from the experiences of others. Because it is so interactive, this technique also requires that you be constantly aware of what is being discussed and of how relevant the information is to the accomplishment of the planned objectives. Therefore, although the small-group session is more informal than other techniques, such as the presentation technique, it is more demanding from your standpoint as a facilitator.

To use this technique effectively, you should do the following:

1. *Listen attentively to what is being discussed.* Since participants are freely communicating with each other, you should monitor what is said in order to prevent misunderstandings and keep the discussion on track. If, when listening to a group, you sense that their discussion is on a topic other than what you had expected, or if there appears to be confusion, you may wish to interject with something like, "John, bring me up to date on where your group is with your discussion." If the group has deviated and has begun to swap stories, this would serve as a gentle encouragement for them to get back on track. If the group members were confused, the question allows the group to give you this feedback. If they are finished with the problem and are waiting for you to reassemble them into the larger group, you can use this feedback and move on to the next portion of the training program.

2. *Remain impartial.* Taking sides in a discussion will alienate some portion of the audience. When you disagree with a point being made, ask a series of key questions that will help the participants evaluate their own answers. Questions such as, "Mary, do you agree with what Tom has just said?" or "Larry, I notice you were shaking your head; do you have a different way of approaching this problem?" will provide opportunities for other people to get involved and give you a chance to hear different sides of the issue.

3. *Provide a proper introduction, summary, and conclusion.* When a larger group is broken up into smaller work units to discuss a given exercise (e.g., a case study), it is necessary for the students to have a good understanding of what the exercise is to accomplish, how much time is available, and in what format the conclusions should be presented (e.g., the group spokesperson presents the findings of the group which have been recorded on a flipchart).

4. *Structure each group so that key knowledge and skill areas are represented.* It is natural for people to want to work with people they know and with whom they feel comfortable. Therefore, it is most likely that individuals will form groups comprised of their friends and/or close associates. Unfortunately, the composition of such a group may not provide the cross-section of knowledge, skill, and experience necessary for the group to reach a proper conclusion for the problem being addressed. To be on the safe side, try to arrange the groups before the session starts, thereby assuring that the proper representation has been achieved.

5. *Control off-track discussions.* You should remain constantly aware of what objectives are to be accomplished and the time available in which to achieve them. If a discussion tends to belabor a point or becomes irrelevant, you must bring it back on track regardless of how interesting the discussion might have been. You can do this simply by saying, "Getting back to the original question . . ."

6. *Circulate among the groups if there is more than one.* If, for example, a fifteen-person group has been broken down into three five-person groups, it is important for you to move from one group to the other. This serves to

   ☐ give the impression to all audience members that you are interested in how well each group is working;

   ☐ provide you with important information which can later be discussed in the large group;

   ☐ identify problem areas and/or misunderstandings;

   ☐ keep each discussion on track.

7. *Guide rather than influence the group's activity.* Because the group will tend to view you as an expert in the material being discussed, students will try to look to you for help in solving problems. If you influence how students deal with given issues, you deprive them of the opportunity to think things through for themselves. In subsequent sessions, when presented with difficult problems, your students may tend to wait for you to tell them how to think and not take this burden of learning upon themselves. You can

reduce the possibility of this occurring by asking a series of questions to help guide the thought process while still giving the students the opportunity to solve the problem themselves. Questions that you can use to guide a group might include "Have you considered your approach from the standpoint of senior management?" or "How do you think our customers would respond to this approach?" or "If you were given this task to do, how would you feel about it?"

8. *Provide positive reinforcement.* Students like to be recognized for their contribution, especially if it is timely, appropriate, or valuable to the overall session. A facilitator who sincerely says "that's a very good question" or "well done" or "that's a good example" provides recognition to the person contributing the thought and encourages others to contribute also.

9. *Be sure the seating arrangement is most conducive to effective group interaction.* Participants should be seated in the group so that eye contact is maximized and each person is an equal to the others. By using U-shaped (also known as a horseshoe) or circle arrangements, you can best encourage participant interaction. A brief discussion of some of the more common seating arrangements is provided in the next section.

10. *Change group assignments where appropriate.* In longer training sessions where a variety of small-group assignments are made, it would be beneficial for both you and your students to vary the composition of the groups. In this way, one person can have the opportunity to interact with many others in the class, thereby expanding the possible number of learning experiences that can be exchanged.

SEATING ARRANGEMENTS

The most commonly used seating arrangements are the U-shape, conference style, theater style, and circle. These are shown in the following diagram.

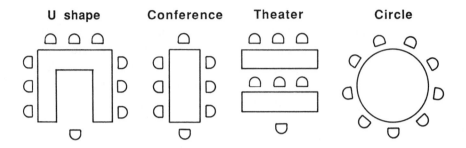

U shape   Conference   Theater   Circle

The U shape is one of the most common seating arrangements used with small groups. It gives you the advantage of being able to move inside the formation to get close to each student, and it provides an opportunity for most students to maintain good eye contact with each other. Some drawbacks are that people sitting along the sides could have difficulty seeing visual aids placed at the front of the room because the person to their side will have his or her head in the way. Also, individuals along the sides will have difficulty maintaining eye contact with others along that same side. A further problem is that the rear of the U shape could be viewed as the group-leader position and may inadvertently give "power" to the person(s) situated there.

This power position is better emphasized in the conference-style setup. Because this is the arrangement most frequently used during business meetings, people tend to expect the group leader to be positioned at the head of the table. Also, by having a table separating the people on the left side from the people on the right, an informal "communication barrier" has been established as one side polarizes itself against the other. The conference arrangement does have the advantage, however, of bringing the group members close together, thereby providing an easy means for members to communicate and share information with one another.

The theater style is not recommended for use with small groups because the disadvantages strongly outweigh any advantages. In this seating arrangement the biggest problem is that eye contact is poor among group members. People in one row have difficulty seeing others in the same row, and individuals in the rear are talking to the backs of the individuals in front of them. The overall effect, therefore, is that the environment is not very conducive to effective group interaction.

The circle format is the most effective arrangement when working with small groups. Eye contact can be maintained with each individual, and there is no informal-leader position. People are close enough together to facilitate discussions with each other, and information can easily be disseminated or shared with other group members.

EXAMPLES FOR IMPLEMENTATION

To illustrate how a small-group process can be integrated into a training session, let's assume that we are working with a ten-person audience and would like to subdivide them into two five-person groups in order to discuss two case studies. The session is scheduled to run two hours.

Training Activity to Be Conducted	Technique Used	Time Involved
Introduction of the session's objectives	Presentation	5 min.
Determination of audience's prior experience with the subject matter	Question-and-answer discussion (large group)	30 min.
Discussion of additional subject material	Presentation	20 min.
Introduction of case-study exercise	Presentation	5 min.
Case-study exercise	Small-group discussion	20 min.
Presentation of each group's findings	Presentation (by group spokesperson)	20 min.
Summary of exercise results	Presentation	5 min.
Clarification of problems, discussion of additional information	Presentation	10 min.
Conclusion, next-day assignment	Presentation	5 min.

This sample training session illustrates that a large group can be broken into smaller work groups to address specific issues provided the time is available in which to do it. By having each group present its findings, the participants get the opportunity to practice public speaking (which is a necessity for professional growth in business today), and it provides a stage from which to communicate the creative and unique solutions the individual groups devised to solve the given problems.

The result is that individuals become more responsible for their own learning and begin to grow as they build a support base from the other members in their group—a support base that will also be available to them once they are back on the job.

Demonstration/Practice Technique

Key points to remember:

☐ Be able to perform the demonstration yourself

☐ Plan the demonstration carefully

☐ Keep it simple

☐ Illustrate with visual aids

☐ Provide opportunity for students to practice

☐ Assign no more than three students to each piece of complex machinery

GENERAL DESCRIPTION

The demonstration/practice technique is a very effective way to transfer learned theory to practical application. This process can be accomplished by having students observe "live" activity conducted by an instructor or resource person or by viewing the demonstration on slides, videotape, or film.

ADVANTAGES AND DISADVANTAGES

Advantages

1. Helps people who learn well by imitating others. Students who learn well by observing and copying the efforts of others benefit most from this technique. By watching the demonstration, these students can form a mental picture

which they can then try to emulate while practicing the desired tasks themselves.

2. Enables students to coordinate sensory input with motor functions through practice. Seeing an activity demonstrated is one thing, but actually doing the activity is something else. This technique therefore provides the student the opportunity to attempt the demonstrated tasks and to get immediate feedback on whether he or she showed an understanding of the concepts and correctly applied those.

3. Promotes self-confidence and builds skills through practice. People have a natural reluctance to trying something new because the consequences of improper action may be unknown or highly exaggerated. Therefore, the more frequently students attempt a task and achieve positive results in a safe training environment, the more likely they will be to use the new skill effectively on the job.

4. Gets students actively involved in the learning process. Skill building is best achieved by having the students become actively involved in the learning process. Tasks that require a high degree of motor skills, such as operating a computer, flying an airplane, or learning the martial arts, cannot just be taught or read about. They also need to be practiced before the desired proficiency level can be achieved.

5. Provides immediate feedback. The opportunity to practice what has been learned provides students with immediate feedback about whether they have properly understood and applied the concepts. When working with a computer, the operator may receive error messages or other strange responses from the machine if the input was incorrect. The operator then knows very quickly where his or her learning and understanding have been deficient.

6. Allows attention to be focused on specific details rather than general theories. General theories are appropriate for providing an overview of a particular subject area. However, when it becomes necessary to operate equipment such as a computer, one needs to concentrate on small, specific details if the functions are to be performed correctly. Trying

to discuss these detailed concepts in a presentation format, however, would be very tedious and time-consuming. Once an individual actually begins performing the tasks, then the specific details can be realistically discussed and acted upon.

Disadvantages

1. Is of limited value for people who do not learn best by observing others. Because this technique relies upon having individuals learn from watching, consideration needs to be given to those who do not respond well to this type of training approach. You may need to conduct remedial work sessions or provide additional reference materials to such individuals in order for the concepts to be fully understood and applied.

2. May not be appropriate for the different learning rates of the participants. Therefore, not everyone will grasp the tasks as quickly as others. Pairing a slower learner with a faster learner is one way of dealing with this problem.

3. Requires specialized expertise if highly technical tasks are involved. Functions such as those relating to the operation of a computer system require that the person who is doing the demonstration be very familiar with the system and ways to handle its various quirks. A person who has limited knowledge about or skill in handling the computer's operation, for example, would find it difficult to respond to technical questions or solve unexpected problems that might occur. In such a case, the overall result could be that the students get a negative impression of the system's capabilities and reliability and, more importantly, lose confidence in the individual who is doing the training.

Pitfalls to Avoid

To be effective in using the demonstration/practice instructional technique, you should avoid the following common pitfalls:

1. Failing to ensure that the students understand the theory before you begin the practice. A good practice session involves application of the theories and concepts that have been taught to real-world situations. If the students do not clearly understand the theory, they will complete the practice by trial and error (based upon memory of what was demonstrated plus pure guesswork). The better students understand the theory, the better equipped they will be to handle the many varieties of problems that they will encounter both in the classroom and on the job.

2. Using the technique to fill time. Each instructional technique has its place, and each should be designed to accomplish a given set of objectives. If a student has demonstrated task mastery after performing three separate problems, it is probably unnecessary to give this individual five more similar problems just because there is time to be filled.

3. Repeating needlessly, so that the students become bored. Each time students practice something, they should either be reinforcing prior knowledge or learning something new. Repetition is good, but you need to recognize when the repetition begins to cause complacency, overconfidence, or boredom. It is part of your training responsibility to keep your audience challenged and motivated.

4. Not being aware of learning plateaus and failing to switch gears to motivate the learners anew. Learning plateaus occur when the amount a student knows and is able to apply no longer seems to increase. In fact, there may actually appear to be a decrease. This may be caused by information saturation, or the individual's weariness with learning. You need to recognize that these plateaus will occur and seek ways to provide further learning motivation.

5. Focusing on problems that do not represent real-world situations. As stated earlier, adult learners want to be able to learn things that can be applied immediately to their jobs. Therefore, to be most effective, the demonstration and practice should tie into real-world situations as closely as possible. Without this real-world focus, the participants' motivation to learn will be short-lived.

KEYS TO EFFECTIVE IMPLEMENTATION

When implementing the demonstration/practice technique, consider the following:

1. *Be able to do what you want to demonstrate.* Few things are more disturbing or embarrassing for an instructor than to encounter a problem during a training session but be technically incapable of correcting it. The more complicated the demonstration, the more likely it is that things will go wrong. Therefore, it is important that you practice ahead of time to be sure you know what to expect and to be able to anticipate potential problem areas.

2. *Carefully plan the demonstration.* The best instruction is well organized. In setting up a demonstration, you need to be sure all equipment is working, the room is arranged so that all participants can observe the demonstration, and the appropriate instructional materials have been copied and are available in sufficient quantities. It would also be helpful, especially with highly technical demonstrations (e.g., with computers), to have a technical resource person either on hand or standing by in the event that serious difficulties arise.

3. *Keep the demonstration simple and the explanation thorough enough to meet your objectives.* It is a common practice for students to take notes as a demonstration is being conducted. You should recognize that this is occurring and move slowly through the demonstration, allowing frequent opportunities to get students' feedback to assure their understanding. The more complicated the demonstration, the more step-by-step the explanation should be.

4. *Augment the demonstration with other visual aids.* Some aspects of a demonstration may be too detailed for everyone to see easily, or the procedure may be too complicated for easy explanation. In such cases it would be appropriate to use other visual aids such as handouts, overhead projections, or flipcharts to help reinforce the points being made.

5. *Give students an opportunity to practice what has been demonstrated.* Doing the demonstration has only succeeded

in proving that you or your subject-matter resource person knows how to perform the tasks. The key, however, is whether the students can apply what they have heard and seen. Through the demonstration the participants get feedback on how well they have performed and on areas where they need to learn more.

6. *Limit the ratio of students using complex machinery (e.g., computer terminals) to a 3:1 ratio.* Thus, each individual can become involved in the learning process more easily, because each can have a role in the practice portion of the session, and each can easily see what the machine is doing. Using the computer-terminal example, when three people have been assigned to one terminal, one can be doing data entry, another conducting the research, and the third can be performing quality checks. In subsequent exercises, these roles would be rotated so that each person has an opportunity to perform all three functions.

EXAMPLES FOR IMPLEMENTATION

The following is a sample session in which the demonstration/ practice technique might be used. The example used is a training class that is focusing on the installation of a new computer system. The session will last two hours and is designed to give students a familiarity with the terminal's keyboard and some of the system's basic functions. During the practice portion of the session, three individuals are assigned to each terminal.

Training Activity to Be Conducted	Technique Used	Time Involved
Introduction of the session's objectives	Presentation	5 min.
Students' concerns about using computers	Question-and-answer discussion	15 min.
Discussion of system's design, capabilities, and limitations	Presentation	30 min.
Overview of computer's basic operations	Presentation	15 min.

63

Training Activity to Be Conducted	Technique Used	Time Involved
Demonstration of basic keyboard functions, log-on/off procedures, and available screen formats	Demonstration	15 min.
Students practice signing on, accessing screens, and logging off the system	Practice	30 min.
Discussion of questions, concerns, and problems	Question-and-answer discussion	10 min.

This example illustrates how the demonstration/practice session can be used with other instructional techniques. It also shows that a demonstration/practice session takes time to complete, especially when the group size is large or the number of terminals is limited. In this example, with three people on each terminal, each person has ten minutes to actually practice the identified tasks. As the work gets more complicated, more time must be allowed for both demonstration and practice.

Case-Study Technique

Key points to remember:

☐ Emphasize analysis of problems not symptoms

☐ Encourage questions

☐ Help students consider alternative solutions

☐ Give a sufficient introduction and conclusion to the exercise

GENERAL DESCRIPTION

A case study is a presentation of facts and/or a representation of a situation to which the student must apply his or her knowledge, experience, and intuition in order to reach a practical solution to an identified problem(s).

ADVANTAGES AND DISADVANTAGES

Advantages

1. May be done in class or as homework. A case study can be a very versatile instructional technique, because it can be used either as an exercise during the actual training session or as homework to be done before, during, or after the session.

2. Provides opportunity to test whether information has been properly understood and can be applied to real-world situations. Because a case study requires a student to apply learned theories and concepts to representative real-world cases, use of a case study immediately enables both you and your students to measure how well the students understand these concepts and can effectively apply them.

3. Can be used with other instructional techniques, in particular, small-group discussions. Case studies can be completed by each student working individually or by students working together in small groups. In the latter situation, the solution to the problem would represent the combined thoughts, ideas, and opinions of several individuals. This further aids in enhancing peer-group learning and the sharing of individual experiences.

4. Enhances peer-group learning through communication of results. Regardless of whether the case study is handled on an individual or group basis, peer-group learning can take place if the students have an opportunity to share their solutions with the rest of the group. This enables individuals to hear how the case was perceived by others and what alternative solutions each might offer. When the case is solved in a small-group setting, one person from the group becomes the group spokesperson and presents the full group's findings.

Disadvantages

1. May encourage oversimplification of the problem under consideration, thereby giving students a false impression of

a situation. Constructing a case study requires the author to have a knowledge of, and a skill in presenting, all the appropriate data upon which alternative solutions can be reached. Hastily developed cases can seriously oversimplify a situation, thereby causing the identified solutions to be only partially effective (or not effective at all) in the real world.

2. May have several solutions to the problem. In addition to developing case studies and similar learning aids, you must develop the "answer keys" to the problems. In this way the instructor has a guide as to what points the case study was designed to address. Many case studies have more than one correct answer, because the broader the problem, the more expansive the potential number of solutions. As the facilitator, you incur the burden of having to listen to all potential solutions and keep an open mind about feasible alternative approaches. These potential solutions can then be incorporated into the answer key.

3. Requires considerable development effort (i.e., time and attention to detail). In developing a good case study, you need to describe the situation, identify the characters, provide the proper forms and reports, and develop an answer key to the problem. If the case study is also going to incorporate the use of complex machinery (e.g., computers), you must also be sure the system is prepared to receive this "test" data.

PITFALLS TO AVOID

When administering a case study during a training session, you should avoid the following:

1. Omitting or not properly correlating important details such as facts and figures. These elements provide the necessary real-world information upon which the students will base their conclusions. Without this detail being available or realistic, the burden falls upon you to invent or modify this data at the time the case study is administered. Frequently, however, this ad-lib approach produces conflicting infor-

mation that alters the way a case needs to be considered or takes precious time during the training session to be resolved.

2. Not having a clear idea of the problem to be solved. Case studies can be fun to use, but they must focus on achieving a defined objective. Case studies that do not have a clear intent merely waste valuable instructional time.

3. Providing insufficient introduction and conclusion to the case-study exercise. No case study should be considered to be the entire instructional effort, but rather part of a larger, more comprehensive lesson plan. Therefore, you should introduce the case study to explain why the case is being discussed, describe how the results are to be presented, and note the time limits involved. Also, you should properly conclude a case study by providing a brief summary of what has been learned.

KEYS TO EFFECTIVE IMPLEMENTATION

To utilize a case study most effectively, you should do the following:

1. *Encourage participants to search for and identify the real problem.* Too frequently, students rely on the apparent problems in order to make decisions. These problems may, however, be only the symptoms of deeper issues. The students need to be encouraged to analyze these symptoms carefully in order to determine whether they are dealing with the actual problem or need to investigate further.

2. *Encourage questions.* In the real world, people are available as resources to others when attempting to solve problems. In order to simulate the real world, try to provide this resource support, where appropriate, during a case-study exercise. This can be accomplished by your serving as a central information source—that is, someone who can provide information that might be available in the real world through telephone calls, memos, and so forth. Such opportunities also can give you an idea of the depth to which each individual or group is approaching a problem.

3. *Help students devise and consider alternative solutions.* While conducting the case-study exercise, circulate among the groups to listen casually to the way each group is addressing the problem. If you see gaps in how an issue is being discussed, ask questions to guide (not influence) the students toward a possible solution. Questions such as "How would the customer view your recommendation?" encourage the participants to consider the solution from another perspective without influencing the process by injecting your own ideas and opinions.

4. *Provide a proper introduction and conclusion.* A good introduction gives the student an idea of why the case study is being used, what it is designed to accomplish, how the results are to be reported, and how much time is available in order to reach a consensus agreement. The conclusion to the case-study exercise should allow you an opportunity to summarize the group findings, to reinforce other key points that may be relevant to the case, and to provide a transition between the exercise and the next topic to be discussed.

ELEMENTS IN WRITING A CASE STUDY

There are essentially two types of case studies: one simulates interpersonal involvement, and the other deals totally with factual data. If you are building a case study that has the element of interpersonal involvement, such as a situation where a student has to determine performance-review recommendations, it would be necessary to include the following in the case-study description:

1. *A description of each of the individuals involved.* This would have to include sufficient details that would normally have been known to the individuals involved in the case. For example, in a performance situation, both the employee and manager would know the results of the employee's work activities, his or her time employed in that position, his or her last performance rating, and so forth.

2. *A description of other people involved.* If other people are involved in the scenario, they too must be described. The details here may not necessarily be known to both parties in

the case study to the same degree. In fact, these elements are frequently the cause of problems in the defined cases. An example might be feedback that a manager has received from another department head regarding the employee's performance but which has never been related to the employee.

3. *An identification of the problem to be approached, underlying criteria, problems that may affect the case, and similar issues.* This should be a clear statement of what is to be resolved in the case and the constraints that can be placed upon a possible solution. Such typical limitations might be budget restrictions, headcount limitations, and so forth.

4. *Specific questions that need to be addressed.* These are the key questions that need to be answered as the individual or group works on the case. By identifying these, each individual or group can devise solutions that will address the same set of questions. Consequently, sharing of information and viewpoints will be easier. In the performance-appraisal example, typical questions might focus on identifying the employee's strengths and weaknesses, needed development efforts, and approaches to dealing with the negative feedback received from the other department.

The following is a sample case study that incorporates interpersonal involvement.

You are the manager of a six-person sales department. You have been with the company five years and are a graduate of their fast-track executive training program. During your training program, you worked in many different areas in the organization, including about one month in sales. You were put in this position when you graduated from the training program six months ago. During this time you have been looking for someone to fill a staff vacancy, trying to complete a comprehensive business plan for next year, and dealing with increasing pressure by your management to meet or exceed an aggressive sales plan (because your boss promised this to his boss).

Joe Rogers has been the company's top salesperson for the last three years, but he has been missing his sales quotas for the last several months. Joe has been with the company eighteen years and until now has always received excellent performance ratings. His consistent production results have often won him sizeable production bonuses. Joe has always appeared to be happy with his job, and the other salespeople look to him for guidance and direction.

Within the past week you have received telephone calls from two of your best accounts complaining about a service problem that your company had promised to remedy. Both of these accounts are Joe's. In addition, the company has a policy stating that "if sales quotas are missed in three consecutive months, the individual will be put on formal warning. Failure to reverse this trend in the next three months will mean termination."

Because it is performance-appraisal time, you feel this is an appropriate time to discuss this feedback with Joe and to determine why his production figures are off. You know that Joe is well respected in the unit and that you will not be able to reach your department's sales objectives without him.

1. What steps would you take in handling this situation?

2. What do you perceive the problem to be?

3. What corrective measures do you think might be appropriate?

When writing a case study that deals with only factual data, such as the implementation of a new computer system, it is necessary to include the following:

1. *A description of the real world.* This sets the stage around which the case study is being built. An example might be a description of what the automated environment is currently like, a description of the new system, and an explanation of what the new system is designed to accomplish.

2. *Necessary forms, facts, and figures.* This would include a complete set of documentation upon which an informed decision could be based. These may be production reports, profit-and-loss statements, or computer input forms.

3. *Availability of supporting materials.* In addition to the material contained in the case study, both you and the students may need to have access to support manuals, the reproduction of which could be cost prohibitive. In such cases, the various manuals relating to computer-system operations should be readily available and in sufficient quantity for everyone (or for every small work group) to use when needed.

4. *Questions to consider.* As with the interpersonal case study, the factual case study must also present the key questions that each person or group needs to resolve. Some typical questions might focus on what the net profit for the organization might be or on the analysis of reports generated by the computer system.

A factual case study would be similar to the interactive case study previously illustrated, except that production reports, staff-performance evaluations, interoffice memos, business plans, and similar appropriate items would be included. Then, based upon this data, the manager might have to develop a series of strategies and action plans for improving sales and meeting plans based on this data. As you might expect, these kinds of case studies are elaborate and take considerable time to develop and administer.

EXAMPLES FOR IMPLEMENTATION

Because the case-study technique is also an aid in the overall communication of the material, its use can best be illustrated as a supplement to an overall topic of discussion. In the following example, the situation is a two-hour training session that represents one segment of a training program in which students are learning how to operate a new computer system and analyze the resulting output. Students will be working on a computer terminal on a 3:1 ratio and have been provided with sample input forms.

Training Activity to Be Conducted	Technique Used	Time Involved
Review of previous session and introduction of objectives for today's session	Presentation	10 min.
Discussion of new computer screens and input/output forms	Presentation	20 min.
Overview of operational requirements	Presentation	20 min.
Introduction to case study	Presentation	10 min.
Problem Analysis	Case Study/Small-group discussion	45 min.
Presentation of results	Presentation (by group spokesperson)	10 min.
Summary of case study, conclusion of session	Review	5 min.

Review Technique

Key points to remember:

☐ Most effective if used with the question-and-answer discussion technique

☐ Use to vary the design of the training session

☐ Use to focus attention on key topics and concepts

☐ Allow sufficient time to use properly

GENERAL DESCRIPTION

The review technique is a systematic means for reexamining the material that has been covered during the previous training segment. Because this technique is predicated on the fact that prior learning has taken place, it should not be used as a means for introducing new information.

ADVANTAGES AND DISADVANTAGES

Advantages

1. Can facilitate information recall. Through the review technique, you have a means of refocusing the student's attention on information that he or she learned earlier.

2. Can help you identify information and/or comprehension problems. Because the technique involves asking the student to describe what he or she has learned, it serves as a feedback mechanism for you. Thus, it enables you to identify areas where more information may be needed or where additional explanation would be required in order to enhance understanding.

3. Provides a bridge between what has been learned in the previous training segments and actual on-the-job applications. This technique can help you bridge the gap between what has been learned and how the information can be used in the real world.

4. Provides an additional opportunity for group participation and interaction. The review technique, if used in conjunction with a question-and-answer discussion technique, can provide you with an additional set of opportunities to get the students involved in their own learning.

Disadvantages

1. Takes time to conduct properly. Asking students to recall what they have learned is a lengthy process, especially if particular items have to be discussed further in order to provide clarification. Of course, a very abbreviated version of this technique would be for you to state what has been learned (using a presentation technique), but this does not contribute to enhancing student participation or providing feedback.

73

2. Can become tiresome and boring for the student if over-used. Once again, too much of a good thing is not helpful. Frequent reviews also have a way of eating up much of the available training time.

3. Can be misused as a means of preparing individuals to take tests. When a review technique focuses the students' attention only on those items that will be tested at a later date, they become aware of this very quickly and soon learn to be attentive only during the last fifteen minutes of a training session.

PITFALLS TO AVOID

To use the review technique effectively, you should avoid the following:

1. Excessively repeating points. Try not to repeat information over and over again to be sure that it is understood. In some cases this may be necessary, but you need to remain aware that such repetition can become boring and tiresome for the students.

2. Using the technique to prepare students for upcoming tests. You may have good intentions, but the result will be a disservice to your students. Students quickly screen information for what they think is important, especially if they know they will be tested on it. If they recognize that your teaching style is to reinforce during the last fifteen minutes of class those points on which they will be tested, this will soon become the only time when your students become attentive.

3. Using the time as a practice session. Practice time should be an integral part of the training session and not reserved for the end of a segment or session. Remember, the intent of the review technique is to reexamine what has been discussed and identify areas of weakness or misunderstanding.

KEYS TO EFFECTIVE IMPLEMENTATION

To use the review technique effectively, you should

1. *use the technique in conjunction with a question-and-answer discussion technique.* This forces the students to continue to be involved in their own learning, and by explaining concepts in their own language, this reinforces the peer-group learning process. Having the students describe their understanding of what has been discussed also provides you with valuable feedback data. Misconceptions or misunderstandings can then be remedied in a timely fashion.

2. *vary the situations when the technique is used.* Using the review technique at key points during the training session will help you vary the overall instructional design and help prevent the onset of boredom among your students. The technique can be used after completion of a major segment or of the entire training session. It can also be used on an interim basis to reinforce key points as the instruction progresses.

3. *focus the students' attention on all the key points and concepts, not just those on which they will be tested.* This promotes a broader perspective of learning and enables you to maintain better the students' attention throughout the entire training program.

4. *allow a sufficient amount of time in the lesson plan for the technique to be used properly.* Conducting a review in conjunction with a question-and-answer discussion technique takes time in order to do it correctly. Therefore, adequate time for it should be built into the lesson plan. The alternative is for you to summarize quickly the key points of what was discussed, but this does nothing to promote group interaction and provides virtually no opportunity for you to measure the students' degree of understanding.

EXAMPLES FOR IMPLEMENTATION

The following might be representative of how a fifteen-minute review could be conducted at the end of a training session using the question-and-answer discussion technique. For the purpose of our example, let's assume the training session involved the introduction of a new computer system, and during this session two objectives were planned and achieved. The first objective was to describe the elements of a computer system and the second was to identify and describe the keyboard and the function of the various keys.

Instructor: What did we say were the main elements of a computer system, John?

John: We said they were ... (let's assume John did not name all of them)

Instructor: Can you add anything to what John said, Mary?

Mary: Yes, there is also ...

Instructor: Very good. We also talked about the keyboard and the functions of several of the keys. What is the "F1" key used for, Bill?

Bill: The "F1" key is used for ... (let's assume Bill's answer is wrong)

Instructor: Do you agree with what Bill said, Kathy?

Kathy: No, the "F1" key is used for ...

Instructor: That's correct, Kathy. Bill, remember that the "F1" key is used for ... You may want to take a look again at page 10 in your manual for additional material on the use of this key.

Instructor: What did we say about the "Help" function, Walt?

Walt: The "Help" function is used to ...

Instructor: Excellent. These are the key points that were discussed. Are there any questions? (Pause) If not, I will see you next Tuesday.

By using a question-and-answer discussion technique to conduct the review, the instructor was able to get the students involved in their own learning, enable them to recall specific points of information, and pinpoint areas in which additional reinforcement was necessary. It also provided an excellent opportunity to provide positive reinforcement to the students when they gave the right answer.

WHAT TO CONSIDER WHEN SELECTING VISUAL AIDS

- Amount and complexity of the information you want to communicate
- Ease in using the visual aid and possibly reusing in another training session
- Whether visual aid can be seen by all students
- Amount of money available to develop visual aids

TYPES OF VISUAL AIDS

- Handouts
- Overheads
- Flipcharts
- Chalkboard
- Slide projector
- Computer terminal

TIPS FOR USING VISUAL AIDS

- Don't read the visual aid to students
- Prepare the visual aid before the training session
- Distribute handouts at the beginning of the session
- Maintain eye contact with the audience
- Pre-check all electrical equipment

VISUAL AIDS

Visual aids are commonly used by instructors to support their presentations. Through the proper use of such aids, you can provide changes of pace in your overall instructional format and provide a graphic display of information to which your students can refer both during and after the training session. Because studies have shown that people remember more of what they see than what they hear, it is important for you to consider how and where best to use visual aids as a means of supplementing your presentation.

Factors in Selecting Visual Aids

In selecting an appropriate aid, you should consider certain factors:

☐ *Amount of information intended to be communicated through the visual aid.* Visual aids should support the instruction; therefore, you should not try to rely on these aids to communicate all the information. Projected (e.g., overhead projector) and displayed (e.g., flipchart) information should be brief and only highlight the salient words or phrases necessary to make a point. Handouts should be considered the primary means for communicating lengthy or complex material.

☐ *Reusability of the material.* If you wish to use the same visual-aid material to support future presentations, you should consider more permanent types of aids such as handouts, slides, or overheads. If the material depends on student input or is susceptible to frequent revision, flipcharts then become appropriate. Flipcharts can also be used to store permanent information, but their size creates a storage problem, and they show their wear easily.

☐ *Complexity of the material.* The more complex the material, the more you should consider developing visual aids, such as handouts, prior to the start of the session. It would be very time-consuming and there would be a higher potential for error if you attempted to discuss complex material while noting extensive information on a flipchart during the training session itself.

- [ ] *Logistical problems.* You should try as much as possible to maintain a smooth transition between the presentation and the visual aids. If their use involves cumbersome movement around the classroom, you should try to find alternative means for communicating the information.

- [ ] *Availability of electrical outlets.* Having a sufficient number of operating electrical outlets is, needless to say, critical to the proper operation of equipment such as overhead and slide projectors. If outlets are unavailable, not operating, or poorly placed (and require several extension cords), alternative visual aids should be considered.

- [ ] *Seating arrangement (or limitations) and the ability of all students to see the visual-aid materials.* If people in the audience are unable to see the aids, then they are ineffective. An experienced instructor pretests her visual aid by viewing it from several locations in the room, especially from the farthest points. If it passes the pretest, it will probably be okay during the session.

- [ ] *Time available to cover the material.* If time is critical, you should consider developing your visual aids prior to the actual session. Handouts, overheads, and flipcharts are especially good for this purpose.

- [ ] *Your own comfort in using the necessary equipment.* If you are uncertain about how to use and operate properly the equipment needed with visual aids, try to avoid learning during the training session, because we all know that is when things are most likely to go wrong. Instead, use the type of aids with which you are most comfortable and seek help in learning how to operate the other equipment for the next time the session is run.

- [ ] *Budgetary considerations.* Putting on a flashy presentation using advanced technology creates an excellent impression with the students, but it could cost thousands of dollars and involve several months of planning and work. Not all operating budgets can support this type of expense. Even the reproduction of a slide-tape program can cost twenty-five dollars per slide. Keep the visual aids simple and the development effort within acceptable time and money parameters.

Types of Visual Aids

In this section we describe some of the more commonly used visual aids and equipment and briefly overview the advantages and disadvantages of using each.

HANDOUTS

Advantages

1. Provide material for the student to refer to both during and after the training session

2. Allow for easy storage, revision, and reproduction of materials for each subsequent class

3. Can be formatted (e.g., typeset, three-hole punched, etc.) as you feel is appropriate and can be bound or placed in a three-ring notebook for distribution

4. Offer a good means for communicating complex or lengthy information

5. Is an excellent means for communicating supporting information that rounds out the discussion of a topic but is not critical enough to need discussion during the training session

6. Can be used to support other visual aids such as overheads, slides, and so forth

Disadvantages

1. Need to be reviewed periodically to assure that it is up-to-date

2. Require revision of outdated materials. Maintenance of lengthy documents could therefore involve considerable effort and time

3. Reproduction quality is limited by the quality of the original. A light original will produce a lighter copy; a blurred original will produce an even more blurred copy

4. When distributed during a training session, virtually ensures that people will want to read the material rather than listen to what is being said

OVERHEADS

Advantages

1. Provide good enlargement of material

2. Allow for easy storage, maintenance, and revision of materials

3. Make possible development of materials either on the spot or before the training session

4. Enable you to use special pens and materials to create multi-colored overheads

5. Enable you, as the instructor, to keep the students' attention focused on a particular page or information segment

Disadvantages

1. Require special equipment (i.e., overhead projector), a large flat surface (e.g., projection screen or plain wall) on which to project the image, and an ability to adjust the room's lighting in order to see the projected image

2. Exaggerate mistakes (e.g., misspelled words)

3. Directly reflect the quality of the original (e.g., a faded original could produce an overhead that is very difficult to read)

4. Require special transparency material (which is relatively expensive) and a machine that can produce the transparencies

5. Can be rendered useless by electrical problems

6. Is subject to equipment availability, especially if the training session is held off-site (i.e., may necessitate the renting of the overhead equipment)

FLIPCHART

Advantages

1. Has the same basic advantages as the overhead but without the enlargement capability (i.e., the information must be drawn on a large scale)

2. Allows for removal and posting around the room of individual sheets for later reference

3. Involves relatively inexpensive materials

4. Does not rely on electricity

5. Can serve as an alternate lesson plan

6. Allows for development of materials either before or during the course of the training session

7. Enables you to emphasize key points easily by using different colors

Disadvantages

1. Makes mistakes clearly visible to the audience

2. Does not allow for easy storage or transport because of its size

3. Can cause frustration if instructors write too small or put too much information on one sheet

4. Can cause you to lose eye contact with your audience if you develop points during a training session

5. Requires legible handwriting

CHALKBOARD

Advantages

1. Provides a large, usually centrally located surface area on which to write
2. Has multicolor capabilities
3. Allows for materials to be developed prior to or during the training session
4. Enables you to revise information easily

Disadvantages

1. Restricts the effective means for retaining the information (i.e., requires note taking before erasures)
2. Offers a limited work surface (i.e., information must be continually erased in order to reuse)
3. Can cause you to lose eye contact with your audience when erasing; and makes it more difficult for the audience to read the information, because erasers do not clean the board very effectively
4. Tends to be very messy because of chalk dust, especially if you are wearing dark clothing
5. With predeveloped material can distract the audience if you are not at a point in the session where the information is to be referenced (since students will tend to read everything they can get their eyes on, especially information they know they are not supposed to be looking at yet)
6. Necessitates legibility, correct spelling, and overall neatness

SLIDES

Advantages

1. Can be used to provide a pictorial history, such as with case studies (e.g., still-frame movies)

2. Can be synchronized with an audio cassette

3. Allow for use of multicolored, professionally developed material from various sources

4. Are easy to store and transport

5. Allow for easy updating by replacing or reordering the sequence of slides

6. Are a good technique if material is not subject to frequent changes

7. Can be used in conjunction with other visual aids

Disadvantages

1. Can be expensive to produce and duplicate (e.g., cost may vary between $25 and $100 per slide depending upon the complexity of the project)

2. Require special equipment that is subject to electrical problems

3. Require adequate time and budget for proper planning, development, and maintenance (an average slide-tape program can take three to six months to plan, develop, and complete)

COMPUTER TERMINAL (CRT)

Advantages

1. Provides students with an opportunity for simulation of real-world situations

2. Provides opportunity for hands-on learning

3. Provides immediate feedback to students on their successes and failures

Disadvantages

1. May involve equipment shortages if production terminals are the only ones available for training purposes

2. Cannot easily transport the equipment

3. May become too costly or unrealistic to set up an off-site system

4. Requires considerable time and effort for development and debugging of practice work; requires the developer(s) to have expertise with the system being used

Using Visual Aids Effectively

As just illustrated, each type of visual aid has its advantages and disadvantages, depending on the type of training situation involved, the time available for training, the complexity of the material, and the budget available for use and production of the visual aids.

Regardless of what visual aid you use, one rule of thumb applies: *do not read the visual aid to the students!!* To be effective when using visual aids give your students the benefit of the doubt that they are able to read the material themselves. Besides, they can read the material silently, two to three times faster than anyone can read it to them. Few things are more frustrating to an audience than to have material continually read to them.

If you feel it is necessary to read the visual aid aloud because of its size or the complexity of the material, it generally means the wrong type of visual aid is being used. If the reading is for purposes of emphasis, an appropriate technique is for you to pause and allow students to read the material and then either paraphrase what it says or ask questions to assure understanding.

When using the different types of aids, you also should remember specific points to help assure that you use the visual aid most effectively.

Visual Aid/Equipment	Operating Tips
A. Handout	1. Whenever possible, distribute the handout material before the training session begins in order to minimize confusion during the session.
	2. Should be used if the extent or type of information to be communicated makes it inappropriate for use through other visual aid technologies.

Visual Aid/Equipment	Operating Tips
	3. Have the material three-hole punched or bound so that it can be easily distributed, carried, and stored.
	4. Use page numbers on all handouts for easy reference during the training session.
	5. Depending on the length of the material, either allow students an opportunity to read the information and then informally test for understanding or inform the students that the information is for reference purposes and is to be read later.
B. Overhead projector	1. Turn on the projection lamp only when the overheads are being displayed; turn it off if there is a lengthy pause between overheads.
	2. Place the acetate on the machine as if you were reading it while facing the audience.
	3. To emphasize a particular item, point to that item on the acetate while it is on the machine using a thin pointer such as a ball-point pen refill.
	4. Maintain eye contact with your audience by first aligning the acetate, making a quick check to see if it is lined up properly on the screen, and then while facing the group, use the acetate as your notes (this avoids continual turning to and from the screen).
	5. Use large enough type so that everyone in the room will be able to read the information.
	6. Mask unnecessary data to minimize distractions.
C. Flipchart	1. Develop complex material before beginning the session.
	2. Set up the flipchart easel where you can reach it easily (depending on whether you are right- or left-handed).
	3. Keep the cap on the marker pens when not in use to prevent their drying out prematurely.
	4. Use a broad-tip marker so that what you write will be large enough for everyone to read.
	5. Maintain eye contact with the audience (avoid the tendency to talk while facing the flipchart).

	6. Plan ahead (leave blank sheets where appropriate).
D. Chalkboard	1. Develop complex material before beginning the session.
	2. Use a clean eraser.
	3. Have a damp towel handy to avoid having to wipe your chalk-covered hands on your clothing.
	4. Maintain eye contact.
E. Slide projector	1. Pretest to be sure everything is functioning normally (including having the right kind of extension cords available).
	2. Know who to call if the machine does not work correctly.
	3. Assure proper orientation of slides.
	4. Use a remote-control slide changer if possible.
	5. Adjust room lighting levels as appropriate.
F. Computer terminal (CRT)	1. Pretest to be sure everything is functioning normally.
	2. Know whom to call if problems occur.
	3. Have an alternate plan if the system is down or machine time is not available.
	4. Limit users to a maximum of three people per terminal.
	5. Be sure technical resource people are available to assist with technical questions.
	6. Determine whether any prerequisite reading has been read and is understood.

TYPES OF LESSON PLANS

- Manuscript
- Sentence
- Topical outline
- Keyword

FACTORS IN ORGANIZING
THE LESSON PLAN SEQUENCE

- Time of day
- Room arrangement and logistics
- Coffee, lunch, and hygiene breaks
- Overall sequence of topics

CHECKLIST FOR PRACTICING
THE PRESENTATION

- Do you have enough time to cover each part of the lesson?
- Does the material flow smoothly from one topic to another?
- Can you use visual aids with a minimum of disruption?
- Is the session organized?

BUILDING AN EFFECTIVE
LESSON PLAN

A lesson plan is any device that you, as an instructor, can use to help organize your training session, to help students remember key points, and to keep you on track. You may find it appropriate to make these notes on 3" × 5" file cards, on standard-size paper, on flipcharts, or on whatever other device you feel most comfortable using.

Every lesson plan has three common elements:

1. The objective that is to be achieved

2. The content that is to be communicated

3. The technique that you feel will best communicate the content

Lesson plans themselves can take any one of four different forms. An instructor will elect to use one or more of these depending upon how comfortable she is with the material. Factors that will influence this comfort level are the following:

☐ *The length of time since the material was last presented.* The more often you present a subject, the higher your comfort level becomes with the content and instructional sequence. The greater your comfort level, the fewer the notes and reminders you will feel are needed.

☐ *The complexity of the material.* More complex material requires more of a step-by-step approach in order to work through the subject's details, therefore the lesson plan needs to be more thorough, especially if leaving a step out could have serious consequences (e.g., defusing a bomb).

☐ *Your personal experience as an instructor.* The less experience you have the longer your lesson plan should be. Experience has shown that most fledgling instructors feel a need to have an abundance of information just in case unexpected questions arise.

☐ *The time frame available for communicating the information.* In situations where time is a critical factor, you will have to rely heavily on a lesson plan to stay on track in order to accomplish the desired objectives.

Types of Lesson Plans

There are basically four types of lesson plans. Each one has its advantages and disadvantages, and whether an instructor elects to use one or more of them in a given training session will depend upon the factors just described.

MANUSCRIPT

The manuscript lesson plan will provide you with the most information possible about a given subject. The material is generally written in paragraph form and is in sufficient depth that most instructors feel comfortable that the large majority of answers to students' questions can be found in this reference.

The manuscript lesson plan is used most frequently with complex information (e.g., where the reasons for each step in a process are clearly spelled out), in training sessions oriented more toward presentation than group interaction, and in situations where the instructor is not very familiar with the material being discussed.

The main advantage of this type of lesson plan is the amount of information that the instructor has at his disposal. By properly researching the subject and structuring the lesson plan in a logical and orderly fashion, an instructor can have a high degree of confidence that he will be able to respond to most questions and concerns. An instructor would then highlight or underline the key-word(s) in each paragraph as a quick visual reference to the paragraph's intent.

The major disadvantage of this technique is that the overwhelming amount of information can create a problem, because locating a specific point within the context of a paragraph is not always easy to do, especially in the middle of a heated discussion. Frustrations with not being able to find needed information quickly may prompt a less experienced instructor to try and "wing it" and hope that her memory was correct.

Another disadvantage is that there is a strong tendency for an instructor to rely totally on the presentation of the information and not allow any opportunity for group interaction. Having someone read you his instructional notes is not usually a stimulating way of conducting a training session.

A manuscript lesson plan also takes considerable time to develop and needs to be neat enough so that it can be easily referenced. Not everyone, however, can remember abbreviations or read cryptic notes several days after the information was written and be certain that he clearly understands the point that was made.

There is also the problem of volume. Because manuscript lesson plans can involve a large quantity of notes, it could be disheartening to students to see an instructor stand behind a podium, open a briefcase, take out a two-inch-thick file folder, and begin reading from it.

Let's assume we are going to teach someone how to drive a car. A sample manuscript lesson plan might look like the following.

Topic	Content	Technique
I. Introduction	Driving a car is a privilege that is extended to us by the authorities in each state. It is therefore our obligation to operate the vehicle in a safe manner. This can only be done if we are aware of the proper techniques for operating the vehicle safely. Our discussion today will focus on the fundamentals of starting up a car and putting it into operation. Tomorrow, we will study the rules of the road.	Presentation (5 min.)
II. Pre-start-up check	Before starting up your car, it is important that you: — adjust your seat to a comfortable position from which you can see forward and reach the control pedals (accelerator, brake, and clutch) — fasten your seat belt — adjust the side and rearview mirrors,	Presentation (5 min.)
III. Starting up	QUESTION: "What steps do you go through when starting up your car?"	Question-and-answer discussion (15 min.)
	Some possible answers might be: — put on the brake to ensure that the vehicle does not	NOTE: Record the responses on a flipchart

```
                    lunge forward and cause
                    potential damage or injury
                 —  if it has a standard shift,
                    depress the clutch and
                    place the shift lever in neutral
                 —  if it has an automatic
                    transmission, place the gear
                    selector in either the "P"
                    (park) or "N" (neutral) position
                 —  place the key in the ignition
                 —  turn the key to the "Start"
                    position and release
```

SENTENCE

A sentence lesson plan is an abbreviated version of the manuscript approach. An instructor who uses this approach determines the key points that need to be made and writes them out in a sentence format. This type of lesson plan is frequently used by relatively inexperienced instructors or by experienced instructors who have not presented the topic within the last six months.

The advantage of this technique is that you can read or paraphrase your sentences as a means for introducing topics, moving from one topic to another, or elaborating on the details of a given subject. The keyword(s) in each sentence can be highlighted or underlined for easy visual reference. Because the lesson plan consists of key sentences, an instructor can be reading her notes without giving that impression to the audience.

The disadvantage of this approach is that in the heat of discussion it may be difficult to find the desired information; and if sentences have been used as transition statements, problems could arise if the discussion in the class takes a different sequential order than planned. In such circumstances, you would have to be comfortable in being able to improvise. Also, because sentence lesson plans can involve a considerable number of cards or sheets of paper, you may need to use a podium. This could inhibit your desire to make a session more informal.

Using the same example as before, the following might be a typical lesson plan that illustrates the sentence format.

Topic	Content	Technique
I. Introduction	* Driving is a privilege (granted by state authorities). * We are obligated to operate a vehicle in a safe manner. * Today's lesson: starting up and operating the vehicle * Tomorrow: rules of the road	Presentation (5 min.)
II. Pre-start-up check	* Adjust the seat for comfort and control. * Fasten the seat belt. * Adjust all mirrors (side and rearview).	Presentation (5 min.)
III. Starting up	QUESTION: What steps do you go through when starting up your car?	Question-and-answer discussion (15 min.)
	Possible responses: — put on the brake — depress clutch and place shift lever in neutral (standard-shift vehicles) — put car in "P" (park) or "N" (neutral) (automatic-transmission vehicles) — put key in ignition — turn key to "Start" and release	NOTE: Record responses on a flipchart

TOPICAL OUTLINE

This type of lesson plan is set up in a standard outline format with major topics identified by roman numerals, subtopics by letters, and so forth. The successive topics and subheadings alternate between numbers and letters.

The advantage of this technique is that it is relatively easy to construct and organize in a logical fashion and can be contained on any size material—3" x 5" cards, 8½" x 11" sheets of paper, or sheets of flipchart paper. Unlike the sentence and manuscript techniques the smaller volume of notes enables you to move away from the podium and get closer to your students. This type of lesson-plan approach therefore lends itself much more to a session that is intended to be interactive.

The disadvantage of this technique is that an outline is only a brief sketch of the subject matter. If you are not well versed in the material or perhaps have not presented the material within the last six months, you may find it difficult to remember all the key points that need to be discussed. As a result, you may have to spend considerable time researching the information in order to refresh your memory.

Another disadvantage is that your outline may be a problem for someone else who may have to present the same subject at a later session. The topical outline represents only one person's idea about how best to discuss a given subject. However, since no two instructors are alike, your instructional style and ideas are probably not the most effective technique or approach for someone else. If others are expected to use the lesson plan at a later date, it would probably be wiser for you to develop a sentence lesson plan rather than a topical outline, even though it will take longer to do.

Again, using the same driver-training example, the following is an illustration of a topical-outline lesson plan.

Topic	Content	Technique
I. Introduction	I. Driving is a privilege A. Granted by state authorities B. Have obligation to operate in a safe manner	Presentation (5 min.)
	II. Training schedule A. Today: start-up and operation B. Tomorrow: rules	
II. Pre-start-up check	III. Steps to follow A. Adjust seat B. Fasten seat belt C. Adjust mirrors	Presentation (5 min.)
III. Starting up	IV. QUESTION: "What steps do you go through when starting up your car?"	Question-and- answer discussion (15 min.)
	(Possible answers) A. Set brake B. Standard shift 1. Depress clutch 2. Shift to neutral C. Automatic transmission 1. Have lever in "P" or "N" D. Key in ignition E. Start	NOTE: Record responses on a flipchart

KEYWORD

A keyword lesson plan identifies only the words and phrases that an instructor feels are necessary to trigger her memory about what needs to be discussed. This type of lesson plan design would therefore be used by individuals who are very knowledgeable about the subject or who have presented the same information with a fairly high degree of frequency within the last six months.

The advantage of this technique is that it is relatively easy to put together. It is also very flexible because if the instructor is already knowledgeable about the subject, she does not have to spend time looking for information, should the discussion get out of sequence. A quick glance at the lesson plan will remind her of what has been discussed and what remains.

Because the entire lesson plan can be put on a single card or sheet of paper, it allows you to give the impression to your students that the training session is being conducted informally. This will provide further encouragement to audience members to participate freely in the discussion.

The disadvantages of this approach are similar to that of the topical outline in that the burden of remembering the details of the information rests with the instructor, and a keyword lesson plan is practically useless to someone else who may be expected to present the same information at a later date.

Continuing with our driver-training example, the following lesson plan illustrates the keyword format.

Topic	Content	Technique
I. Introduction	* Privilege * Obligation for safe operation * Training schedule	Presentation (5 min.)
II. Pre-start-up check	* Seat * Seat belt * Mirrors	Presentation (5 min.)
III. Start-up	QUESTION: "What steps do you go through when starting up your car?"	Question-and-answer discussion (15 min.)
	(Possible answers) * Brake * Clutch/shift (standard shift) * Park/Neutral (automatics) * Key * "Start" position	NOTE: Record responses on a flipchart

Practice and Evaluation

The key to building an effective lesson plan is to select the format or combination of formats with which you are most comfortable; to practice presenting the material; and to evaluate critically whether you, as your own average student, think it would make an effective training experience for your audience.

As you practice try to ensure the following things.

- ☐ *The plan is practical and achievable within the given time frames.* You run a high risk of failure if you try to do too much in too short a period of time.

- ☐ *The timing of the activities is correct.* For example, planning a case study that involves intense small-group activity to be done in ten minutes would be inappropriate, because such an exercise will most likely last a minimum of thirty minutes (if it is to be done correctly).

- ☐ *Material flows smoothly from one subject to another.* Material presented in a disorganized manner can be frustrating and confusing for students. To be an effective facilitator, you should be sure that smooth transition statements take the lesson plan from one topic to another.

- ☐ *Gymnastics involved in using equipment are minimized.* Limit the use of visual-aid equipment to perhaps one or two different devices during a training program. For example, trying to distribute handouts, write on flipcharts, use an overhead projector, and operate a slide projector all during the same session can provide comic relief to the audience as they take bets on how long it will take before you trip over an extension cord.

- ☐ *The session is organized.* This is the last chance for you to identify whether additional reference, handout, or other visual-aid materials are needed: to determine whether other resource people need to be consulted; and to anticipate other questions or problems that may be encountered.

After practicing the material, you should give yourself a very thorough critique of your lesson plan. By evaluating the session from the standpoint of your students, you can begin to anticipate how they are likely to react. When doing this self-critique, consider how you would like to have learned this information. If something does not feel right, change it.

As you go through the material, think about what is being communicated. If you can continually answer the question "So what, who cares?" with a specific and positive response, then you can be well assured that the information being discussed will be important and that the probability of the training program's success will be high.

Organizing the Lesson-Plan Sequence

To be effective, a lesson plan must be arranged with a logical sequence of events. To do such arranging, however, you must be aware of certain factors such as the time of day when the material will be discussed, the room layout and logistics, time allocations for coffee and lunch breaks, and the overall sequence of topics to be covered.

TIME OF DAY

When building a lesson plan, the time of day becomes a critical element. Studies have shown that between 8:00 and 9:00 A.M. people generally are moving in slow motion, trying to get themselves organized for the day ahead. From 9:00 to 10:30 A.M. individuals are working at their best. From 11:30 to 1:00 P.M., most people become mentally preoccupied with lunchtime activities. Between 1:00 and 2:00 P.M. a postlunch mental depression occurs. Between 2:00 and 3:30 P.M. individuals have gained their second wind and are working again near capacity, and between 3:30 and 5:00 P.M. people begin to think about going home or about after-work plans.

If you are aware of this phenomenon, you can use it to your advantage. Highly interactive techniques, such as the question-and-answer discussion technique, work well in the early morning and early afternoon to get students mentally stimulated for the rest of the session. Group exercises are effective for the midmorning and midafternoon times when people are most alert. Presentations can work well in the latter part of the morning and afternoon, because they can best be adjusted to lunch breaks and quitting times.

You want to avoid scheduling presentations right after lunch in a darkened, warm room where overheads or 35 mm slides will be used extensively. Otherwise, when the lights come back on, you may find your students asleep. Also, avoid the use of interactive exercises, such as case studies, at the end of the day. Students' concerns about after-work obligations could cause them to rush through the project assignment and therefore not derive the intended benefit from it.

ROOM ARRANGEMENT AND LOGISTICS

If a lesson-plan activity calls for the group to subdivide into smaller groups, you need to make an adequate time allowance in the lesson plan for this change to take place. In addition, time must also be allowed at the end of the exercise for the group to reassemble. This would be especially important if the smaller groups are assigned breakout rooms some distance away from the main meeting room.

Another consideration would be the physical layout of the room. If small groups are to be formed by physically dividing the main meeting room with sliding partitions or by reorganizing the total seating arrangement, adequate time should be allowed for the assembly and disassembly. This can usually be accomplished by having such activities occur around coffee or lunch breaks. If the session is being held in an off-site facility, arrangements can usually be made with facility-maintenance personnel to assist in this process.

COFFEE, LUNCH, AND HYGIENE BREAKS

Few things are more disturbing and disruptive to an audience than the threat of missing a morning coffee break. An appropriate time for scheduling this would be between 9:00 and 10:00 A.M., depending on when the preceding session began. A similar type of break should be scheduled for midafternoon.

In consideration of these opportunities to have coffee, tea, or whatever, hygiene breaks should be scheduled every hour. We probably all can relate to the discomfort of having to sit and listen to someone for an extended period of time after having had several cups of coffee. These frequent breaks also allow you, as the instructor, to change the pace of your presentation by allowing people to stretch their legs and to relax mentally for a few minutes.

Coffee breaks generally last fifteen to twenty minutes, and the normal lunch break lasts approximately one hour. By taking into consideration these planned disruptions, you should be able to schedule your presentations and exercises accordingly.

TOPIC SEQUENCE

Although this consideration may appear to be obvious, too many of us have encountered situations in which the instructor erroneously believed that the necessary prerequisite material had already been discussed. This is especially important when more than one instructor is involved in presenting a training program. In situations that require some degree of prior knowledge, you must be sure that the necessary information has been adequately addressed. If not, you may have to spend additional time in order to lay the proper foundation for your students.

HOW TO PRESENT A SUCCESSFUL TRAINING SESSION

- Check the room and materials ahead of time
- Make sure your appearance is appropriate
- Start promptly
- Remember the first five minutes set the tone
- Greet people as they enter
- Speak confidently and with respect
- Look for a friendly face
- Become aware of any distracting mannerisms
- Use a podium or pointer appropriately
- Be willing to change your approach or material to meet the needs of the students
- Affirm student responses
- Plan introductions of other presenters
- Don't make excuses

TIPS FOR MAKING EFFECTIVE PRESENTATIONS

Once you have determined what instructional technique(s) is (are) best suited to accomplishment of a given objective and you have planned the lesson, it is up to you to present the material properly. Virtually all trainers are a little nervous before going in front of a new group of people, but an effective facilitator minimizes this concern by being adequately prepared and confident that the training session will represent his best possible effort. To make this happen, there are several things that should be considered.

Keys to Effective Presentations

KNOW THE ROOM AND MATERIALS

You can minimize your anxiety by familiarizing yourself with the logistics of the presentation. You should ensure the following things:

☐ You are aware of the room's layout and facilities. This would include knowing the location of light switches, power outlets, audiovisual support devices (e.g., remote-control slide changer, rear-screen projector, automated projection screen). You should also know how to adjust the room temperature and outside lighting.

☐ The training room can properly support the exercises and techniques to be used. For example, a conference room may have a single large table that would have to be worked around if the large audience is to be occasionally broken up into smaller work groups.

☐ You know how to properly operate (and troubleshoot) the visual-aid equipment to be used.

☐ The training material has been properly organized, and sufficient copies are available for all attendees.

CHECK PERSONAL APPEARANCE

To be an effective facilitator, you should look critically at yourself. Your attire should be consistent with the atmosphere of the session. An instructor who elects to wear a three-piece suit in an informal mountain-lodge setting may give the audience a negative impression of his message.

Another element is your personal appearance. Just before the session, look in the mirror and critically judge whether everything you see is satisfactory. A coffee stain, messy hair, or an unbuttoned shirt provides unnecessary distraction.

BEGIN ON TIME

The training program's agenda was developed for the purpose of accomplishing a given set of objectives within a defined period of time. If the session is scheduled to begin at 8:30 A.M. and you are the first instructor, it is your obligation to begin the program on schedule. A fifteen-minute delay in getting started, a five-minute delay in beginning after the morning and afternoon breaks, and a ten-minute delay in starting up after lunch will have taken away thirty-five valuable minutes of training time.

CREATE A POSITIVE FIRST IMPRESSION

The impression you make as a facilitator will be primarily determined by how well you come across to the participants during the first five minutes of your session. If you are late, disorganized, willing to make excuses for the session or materials, and so forth, then you have to expect that a long uphill battle is ahead of you if your desire is to provide a positive learning experience for your students.

ESTABLISH A COMFORT LEVEL WITH THE AUDIENCE

As was mentioned earlier, it is normal to be a little nervous before a new training session begins. If you are the first person on the agenda in the morning or are scheduled to begin immediately after a coffee or lunch break, you may try to alleviate this anxiety by situating yourself near the entrance to the training room and greeting people as they walk in. If nothing else, this technique gives you an idea of what the audience looks like, and it will help enable you to get a first impression about the group from how they respond to your greeting. Once the session starts, you can then look to those with the friendly faces and create a solid base upon which to build the rest of the session.

USE AN APPROPRIATE TONE OF VOICE

The tone of voice you use can significantly contribute to—or detract from—your effectiveness during a training session. All members of the audience expect to be treated equally and respected for the knowledge and skills they bring into the classroom. Being condescending discredits people who may not have the same experiences as others and may polarize some class members against the instructor or other attendees. In addition, your tone of voice should reflect the message being communicated. If the message is that you are encouraging openness, but your tone of voice reflects mistrust and doubt, it is unlikely that the communication will be 100 percent effective.

Effective facilitators also strive to eliminate or minimize the use of "ums" and "ahs" when speaking. I know of at least one class that became so enthralled by the instructor's persistent use of these "words" that the class members covertly organized a contest to guess how many times he used these in a single training class. The result was that more people listened for his distracting habit than for the information being discussed.

FIND A FRIENDLY FACE

Most of us have had situations in which the person to whom we are talking nods his or her head in a positive manner as we speak. The conclusion we draw from this behavior is that this individual agrees with what we are saying and will support us if a question should arise. You can use this and similar types of positive nonverbal behavior to your advantage in a training situation.

People who exhibit these types of behavior are called "friendly faces" and can give you a clue about how well you are presenting the material and making on-target points.

For example, if you are beginning the discussion of a new subject, and you want participants to share their experiences, you would look for the individuals who are nodding their heads or smiling. Your initial questions could then be directed to these individuals, because they have a higher probability of knowing

108

the answer or providing supportive comments. Thus, using the friendly face approach provides a positive means for introducing material, getting participants involved, and providing positive reinforcement to others that it is safe to contribute their thoughts and ideas.

AVOID DISTRACTING MANNERISMS

Few things can affect an instructor's effectiveness more than the unconscious use of distracting mannerisms. Although the information being discussed may be extremely interesting, the effectiveness of the presentation can be tarnished by the fact that the audience has become disturbed by the facilitator's mannerisms. Habits such as jingling pocket change, playing with jewelry, making wild and erratic hand gestures, pacing constantly, and using negative nonverbal behaviors (e.g., folded arms, raised eyebrows) can detract from an instructor's effectiveness. A good way of overcoming these problems is to have a friend evaluate a mock presentation or to have a practice session videotaped and critiqued. Rehearsing in front of a mirror will give you some self-feedback, but its overall value is limited because of the lack of an independent opinion.

USE A PODIUM OR POINTER TO SUPPORT
THE PRESENTATION

In addition to the various visual aids that are available, there are two other devices that, if used properly, can contribute to an instructor's effectiveness: a podium and a pointer. Like so many other things in training, their effective use naturally blends in with the rest of the presentation and enhances the session's overall effectiveness. When they are used correctly, no one ever notices it. However, their misuse tends to stand out like a sore thumb.

A podium is generally used with groups of eight or more people and in an atmosphere where a more formal learning environment is to be maintained. A podium is designed to hold notes at an angle to facilitate easy reading and reference. It can, however, be misused if the presenter leans on it, hides behind it, grasps it too tightly, or places a thicker quantity of notes on it than can be supported. In the latter case, this could result in the instructor's notes falling to the floor—a definite problem, especially if the notes are on 3″ × 5″ cards and not sequentially numbered.

A pointer is a device used to direct the audience's attention to a given piece of information that appears on the wall, flipchart, projection screen, or other surface. The pointer can be misused—as a cane, sword, baton, golf club, pool cue, and so forth. Leaders who use the pointer in such creative but inappropriate ways are sure to distract their audience.

ADJUST THE MATERIAL TO THE AUDIENCE'S LEVEL

Situations will inevitably arise in which you miscalculated the background and/or experience level of your audience. Also, as you gain experience in facilitating training sessions, you will begin to find that groups seem to take on personalities of their own and that the techniques that worked effectively with one group do not necessarily work well with another. During the course of the session, you may find that the audience knows more (or less) about the subject than you originally anticipated; to be effective, you then need to change the program. Such alterations may entail the following:

☐ Adjusting the language level of the material being presented. The use of advanced concepts or material that requires prerequisite knowledge could be disastrous if you find the audience unready for this level of detail.

☐ Sitting down with the group rather than standing in front of them. You may feel that you can be more effective with a group if a less formal training setting is used or vice versa.

☐ Altering the frequency and depth of questions. For example, if the audience demonstrates a lower level of knowledge and/or skills than you expected, the strategy for using questions may have to be altered in order to focus on assuring understanding of the concepts being discussed rather than on measuring how the concepts could be applied and the consequences of ineffective application.

☐ Changing the instructional-style "game plan." The technique(s) used should properly balance the knowledge and

110

skill levels of the audience, the objectives to be achieved, the time available for training, and the complexity of the material.

☐ Adding words, phrases, or examples that enhance the understanding of the material. Many people will learn concepts better if they have concrete examples of how a theory has been applied in actual practice.

PROVIDE POSITIVE REINFORCEMENT OF RESPONSES

When individuals make positive contributions during a training session, their involvement should be recognized and further encouraged. By providing some type of positive reinforcement, you also signal to others in the audience that their ideas are valuable, that all ideas are welcome, and that people should not have a fear of criticism regarding the ideas they wish to offer. Your appropriate and sincere use of comments such as "good example" or "that's a very interesting point" or "excellent" can have long-lasting value.

INTRODUCE YOURSELF AND OTHER PRESENTERS SMOOTHLY

During training programs that last more than a couple of hours, it is not unusual to have two or more individuals giving presentations. Sometimes the transition from one presenter to another can take place over a coffee break or lunch, but more often it occurs in the middle of the morning or afternoon. The better this transition can be made, the more professional the impression that is given to the audience. To accomplish this smoothly, talk briefly with the person who may be introducing you and provide him with a general idea of what can be said for an introduction. Do the same thing for individuals you will be introducing. Information such as who you are, your department, and why you have been asked to speak provide your introducer with a good place to begin.

NEVER MAKE EXCUSES

How do you feel when an instructor says, "I normally do this session in three hours, but I've been asked to cover this same material in an hour, so let's get started" or "This is the first time I've taught this" or "Please ignore all the spelling and typographical errors in the handouts; I had to put this together in a hurry"? The immediate impression is that the instructor did not care enough about the program to take the necessary time to do it well. As a member of the audience, you have been primed to think of the session as being second-rate, and unless a miracle occurs, that is exactly how you will view the session when it ends. Although the session may have been good, your first impression of the instructor and your overall perception of the program gave you the feeling that you were short-changed.

To be an effective facilitator, you should go into a training session feeling confident about the objectives to be accomplished, your ability to use the planned techniques, and the materials to accomplish these objectives. An instructor who feels this way never has to make excuses for the program, the material, or the techniques and exercises used.

HOW TO CHOOSE AND INVOLVE
SUBJECT-MATTER RESOURCES

- Determine how and where a SMR can help the training process
- Identify who would be the best SMR for the program
- Negotiate with the SMR's manager for support
- Explain specific roles and responsibilities of the SMR
- Request updates from SMR on the planning and development
- Give constructive feedback

USING
SUBJECT-MATTER RESOURCES

A subject-matter resource (SMR) is anyone who is able to demonstrate a high degree of technical knowledge about, and/or skill in being able to perform, a particular set of tasks. This expertise may have been acquired through time on the job or through a concentrated period of study in the particular area. Many trainers refer to such a person as a subject-matter expert (SME), but because there are few true experts in this rapidly changing and complex world, we find the term subject-matter resource to be more accurate.

The sources and types of SMRs are unlimited. For example, an instructor who is building a training session that will focus on the development of various management skills such as planning, organizing, controlling, making decisions, and interviewing may find it useful to have available a variety of different individuals who have been recognized by their peers and managers as being very competent in one or more of these areas. In another case, such as when a training program is being designed to introduce a new computer system, it would be valuable for an instructor to solicit the assistance of individuals who are technically proficient in the new system (e.g., programmers, a project manager) and who could be available to answer detailed questions regarding the system, should they arise.

Ways to Use
Subject-Matter Resources

You can use SMRs in any one (or in a combination) of four different ways:

1. To provide technical input into the design of the training program and the materials that will be used during the session (e.g., handouts, case studies)

2. To be available on call while the training program is in session

3. To be available in the classroom during the actual training session to respond to questions and provide clarification where needed

4. To conduct all or part of the training session

Your best use of a SMR will depend on the individual's ability and experience with designing and developing training materials and programs, as well as her comfort level with doing actual facilitation. These skills can be determined through discussions with her manager, through others who have used the SMR in similar capacities in the past, and through actual discussions with the individual who has been identified as being a good SMR.

Identifying and Securing the Assistance of the SMR

SMRs usually come out of a support area such as data processing or financial services, and, for many of them, having to help design and/or facilitate a training program is not normally considered part of their job description. It therefore becomes very important for you, as the instructor in charge, to use the utmost tact and corporate diplomacy to secure this necessary assistance.

The key to success in securing the cooperation and support of a SMR is effective communications. You should pay close attention to such details as who needs to be included in the request-and-approval chain; how long the person can be committed to the project; how many estimated person-days of effort are involved; what the SMR will be expected to deliver, what target date(s) is involved; and what the SMR's specific role and responsibility will be before, during, and after the training program.

For the purpose of this discussion, let's assume that even though you are from a technical area, you feel there is a need to have additional resource support available to fill in certain gaps in your own background, knowledge, or skills. In seeking to identify an appropriate SMR, your first step then would be to determine which of the program's objectives requires that a SMR be involved. You will then need to ascertain how a SMR can be used most effectively to accomplish these objectives.

Once this has been done, you can begin the search for the appropriate resource people. If SMRs have been used in the past, discussions with other instructors can provide evaluative feedback on

117

each individual's strengths and weaknesses. It might also be useful to read student evaluation forms of prior training sessions to get some additional insight into who has been most or least effective.

After identifying who would serve as a good SMR, you then have the job of negotiating with the SMR's manager for the needed time. It is important that this step be taken prior to having any discussion with the intended resource person, because a morale problem could be created if the SMR agreed to do the requested work but later found out that the manager felt she could not be made available because of work priorities, overall work volume, a determination that she may not have the needed knowledge and/or skills, or similar such reasons. You can avert such problems by talking to the manager first.

Once the manager has approved your use of the resource person, and the SMR has scheduled the time on her calendar, it is important for you to provide a written confirmation to the SMR's manager of all of the details to which you and the resource person have agreed. Although this process will not eliminate all potential problems, having such an agreement available will minimize the potential for disagreements and memory lapses in the future.

Your task now is to work with the SMR to clearly specify what her roles and responsibilities will be for the training session. It is also much easier to get the SMR's cooperation now, because the approval to use her has come from the manager on down. During this stage of the process, you should make clear when and where the session will be held; what you expect her to do; the target dates that need to be met; and, because this individual is probably not a skilled training-program or materials developer, whom she can use as a resource person to be sure that the material being developed will be effective in a training environment.

If part of the SMR's role will be to conduct only certain segments of the training program, you should be sure the SMR understands what has been discussed prior to her segment and what will be covered afterward. You should also review with the SMR who will be in the audience, their respective strengths and weaknesses, and known problem areas (e.g., an individual who likes to hear himself talk, two people who may not get along well). In addition, you should volunteer to provide any train-the-trainer assistance should the individual feel that she would like to practice before the session.

As a means of quality control, you should request periodic updates from the SMR on how well the development of the materials or lesson plans is proceeding. If you find that, because of other work pressures, the SMR's development effort is beginning to fall behind schedule, the problem can be identified sooner, her manager appropriately kept up to date, and corrective action taken more effecively.

Developing training materials, lesson plans, and so forth takes time, especially for someone who is not accustomed to doing it. It is not unusual for the development process to take up to six months to complete if more complex material is involved or if the material being presented is new or unfamiliar to the instructor. Therefore, when you ask for other people's assistance, you need to take this development time into account. If possible, target the completion date for the SMR's work to a minimum of two weeks in advance of the scheduled date. This will allow you ample time to review the entire content for consistency, effectiveness, typographical errors, and so forth and to have a sufficient number of copies of support materials made for the attendees.

On the day before the session that the SMR is scheduled to attend, it would also be appropriate to call and remind her of the time and location of the training session. This will help you avoid a potential embarrassment by having an entire class waiting for a SMR who, because of an honest mistake, forgot about the session (or wrote down the wrong date or time on the calendar) and who is out of the office, attending another meeting, or otherwise unavailable.

Following Up the Training Session

Of equal importance to having the SMR become involved in the planning, preparation, and facilitation of a training session is conducting a follow-up with the SMR once the session has concluded. First, you should send a sincere note of thanks to the individual, with a copy of the letter going to her manager. Not only does this provide input that the SMR can use at performance-evaluation time, but it also helps build a positive working relationship between you and that technical resource area.

You should also review the students' evaluation forms and communicate the findings, both positive and negative, to the SMR. In this way both you and the SMR have a basis on which to build the next time she is asked to serve as a SMR.

If problems have been identified with the material (e.g., case study, handouts) that the SMR developed, she should update the material as soon as possible after the training session is over. In this way the information will still be fresh in her mind, and a minimum of additional research will be necessary. It will also be easier to get a commitment from her manager if you request that the corrective work be done as soon as possible after the session, because her manager will more likely perceive this request as an extension of the current training session and not resource support for a subsequent one.

In the next chapter we discuss more about evaluating a program's effectiveness and techniques for providing constructive feedback.

METHODS OF PROGRAM EVALUATION

- Paper-and-pencil tests
- Case studies
- Observing students back on the job

HOW TO IMPROVE A TRAINING PROGRAM

- Change the program's objectives or content
- Help guest instructors improve their training skills
- Replace ineffective instructor
- Give remedial work to students

HOW TO GIVE CONSTRUCTIVE FEEDBACK

- Give factual data with feedback
- Ask questions
- Listen carefully
- Reinforce what the person is doing well
- Have practical suggestions for improvement
- Share results with the individual's manager if appropriate

EVALUATION AND FEEDBACK

Perhaps the most difficult—and yet the most crucial—aspects of the training process are evaluating the effectiveness of the training, knowing the appropriate corrective action to take, and being able to provide constructive criticism to individuals who may be performing below desired training standards.

Each of these elements is rooted in the initial objectives that you established for the training program, and each provides additional evidence that you should place considerable importance on effective design of a training program. The evaluation of a student's progress must be measured in terms of how well an objective has been attained. When you take a corrective action, you need to focus on why an objective may have been missed and what further corrective action is necessary to bring the training program back on course. Providing constructive criticism enables you to address specifically what learning objectives the student missed and what remedial work may be appropriate to overcome this shortfall.

Even though you may technically only be considered a part-time trainer, the task of evaluating a training program's effectiveness and giving constructive feedback may be part of what is expected of you on the job.

Ways to Evaluate a Program

There are several different options available by which you can measure the effectiveness of either an entire training program or a segment of it. These options include

- ☐ paper-and-pencil tests
- ☐ participation on case studies
- ☐ on-the-job observations of actual work activities

Each of these evaluative approaches has its strengths and weaknesses. Let's look at each one individually.

PAPER-AND-PENCIL TESTS

It is not easy to develop a good written test. Each question on the test must be clearly stated, meet an identified program objective, and require a student to use knowledge and/or skill that he has learned (or developed) during the training program.

There are essentially three kinds of paper-and-pencil tests:

- ☐ the narrative (essay)
- ☐ short answer (fill-in-the-blank)
- ☐ multiple-choice questions

Narrative (Essay) Tests

The narrative test generally asks students to recall and bring together many different facts and concepts they learned during the training program. Because of this, an essay question is usually broad in scope. This, however, presents a significant challenge for you, as the instructor, or for your SMR in that the answer key for such a broad type of question takes time to develop and must be comprehensive in order to address the different aspects from which the question can be viewed.

The broad nature of both the question and its potential answers also affects how you evaluate whether a student knows the answer. Because no two students will answer a narrative question in exactly the same way, you must use some subjective judgment in grading these types of tests. This subjective element also provides you with the greatest degree of latitude for determining whether the student has adequately learned the desired material.

A sample narrative question might be: Based upon the economic factors discussed during this training program, what do you see as the major challenges facing our company next year?

Short-Answer Tests

The short-answer type of test asks the student to recall specific bits and pieces of information. Therefore, a short-answer test is closely aligned with the material used during the actual training program. The answers to short-answer tests may range from only one word to a key phrase. As a result, these types of tests are both relatively easy to construct (i.e., they closely follow the instructional material) and to grade (i.e., the instructor can be very objective in determining whether an answer is correct).

One disadvantage of this type of test is that it could compel the student to memorize facts and then try to guess exactly which words or phrases you wanted for answers. Another potential disadvantage is that you need to avoid the trap of directing your teaching toward the test. Virtually all instructors want to walk away from a training session with a feeling that their students learned what they were supposed to and that this achievement is measurable on some form of evaluation. Because instructors know how their training will be measured, there is a strong temptation to emphasize only those points that will be covered on the short-answer tests. Although this tactic will probably produce high grades, it hinders students from paying serious attention to important related facts on which they will not be tested.

A sample short-answer question might be as follows: *Each computer system includes pieces of* _____ *and* _____.

Multiple-Choice Questions

The multiple-choice question asks students to recall facts and make judgments as to which one of several possible responses best answers a given question. This type of test is very easy to grade because the correct answer will be one of those identified on the test; there is no subjective judgment needed.

However, designing a good multiple-choice question is not easy. Usually, multiple-choice questions will have four possible choices. This reduces the "guess factor" to 25 percent. In addition, each of the choices should at least be plausible alternatives, because having ridiculous choices that can be quickly eliminated raises the potential for good guessing to 33 or even 50 percent. Coming up with the right answer plus three good choices is your greatest difficulty in building a multiple-choice test.

When designing multiple-choice tests, you must also be careful to measure all the appropriate learning objectives that you covered in the training session. For example, if a training segment covered three objectives, but the test only measured two of them, the results could only be considered partially accurate. One or more additional questions would need to be developed to fill this gap.

A sample multiple-choice question is as follows: *A disk drive is considered part of a computer's: (a) hardware (b) software (c) peripheral equipment (d) none of the above.*

PARTICIPATION ON CASE STUDIES

Case studies are also excellent means for evaluating whether a student has successfully comprehended the training material. The case study (which was described in chapter 4) is designed so that students can analyze real-world situations and apply what they have learned.

Through the discussion of solutions to the individual cases, you should be able to ascertain the depth to which an individual or a group is able to handle a problem. Because the problems are being analyzed in a safe, nonthreatening environment, you should encourage your students to take risks. The results of this type of measurement device will provide you with valuable insight into the creative potential of your students.

Case studies, however, have the drawback of requiring time to complete effectively and of being difficult for you or your SMR to evaluate, because the assessment of each requires a substantial amount of subjective judgment. Frequently, a complete answer to a case study will represent a composite of the different viewpoints expressed by the students.

If each person is to analyze a case study, and there are ten people in a class, you would have to critique ten possible responses. This would then become akin to the problems identified earlier in this section with the narrative type of test. If you elected to have the solution(s) to the case study resolved in a group, the responses would be fewer, but it would be impossible for you to determine how each individual member comprehended the information because the result would represent a consensus of the group's ideas and opinions.

ON-THE-JOB OBSERVATIONS OF ACTUAL WORK ACTIVITIES

No training situation can simulate all possible problems that you will encounter on the job. In fact, it is unrealistic to expect that any one training program can be designed to cover all these potential problems. Therefore, when a program is designed, it has to focus on those problems that are most likely to occur and those that will have the greatest effect on the ability of an individual to perform his job.

Use of the demonstration/practice instructional technique can highlight whether students have learned the fundamentals while in the classroom, but what happens on the job can provide insight into whether additional training should be conducted or whether there are areas in which remedial training may be appropriate. By observing an individual on the job, you will have opportunities to identify such things as system input errors, telephone calls which are not handled appropriately or how well the individual interacts with fellow employees and outside customers. Problems in any one of these areas may give you insight into where the student may not have fully grasped the information or where the training program's content may have to be bolstered.

It is not always easy to do on-the-job observations, however. If you are from outside the functional area where the individual works, there are corporate (i.e., political) chains of command that must be recognized and adhered to in order to get permission to conduct these evaluations. Also, the observation needs to be done discreetly so that the individual does not feel he is working in a "fishbowl" where observation of a series of his errors could affect his job security.

To be effective, observations should be planned ahead of time with some specific evaluative objectives in mind. In addition, the individual's manager needs to "sign off" on allowing the observation to take place over an agreed-upon period of time. The individual being observed should also be aware that the evaluation is taking place, when it will occur, what it is designed to accomplish, and who, if anyone, will see the results of the observation.

It is very important that you emphasize to both the manager and the employee that the observation is being conducted to improve the quality of the training program and to provide professional-development guidance to the individuals who have gone through the training program. You must make it very clear that such observations are not going to be used as a "spying" vehicle for the manager to gather performance-evaluation information about the employee. The element of trust is very important to the success of this process.

128

Ways to Take Corrective Action

As stated earlier, there may be times when the scope of a technical trainer's responsibility for a training program ranges from its design and development phases through its evaluation and maintenance. In the event that part of this accountability includes the evaluation of the program's instructors (e.g., SMRs), then you also need to be in a position to recommend and take corrective action where needed.

The results of the training-program evaluation may either indicate that the desired learning has taken place or that some change is necessary. The corrective action may need to focus on the training program itself, the effectiveness of "guest" instructors, SMRs who may have been used, or the students. In such circumstances, there may be a need for one or more of the following:

☐ Changes to be made in the training program itself

☐ The instructor to receive additional presentation-skills training

☐ A different instructor who can present the material more effectively during the next session

☐ Remedial work for certain students in specifically defined areas

CHANGE THE TRAINING PROGRAM

Weaknesses in the training program itself may be the result of objectives that are too broad, too narrow, or inappropriate; inadequate explanation; or the use of out-of-date material and information.

Changing a program's objectives is probably the most difficult of the three to accomplish because these formed the basis upon which the program was originally created and upon which all the instructional materials were based. At the very outset, in designing the program, the client verified these objectives. If one or more objectives are suspect, you should be prepared to offer a strong argument and definite recommendations as to what needs to be changed, why the change is necessary, the resource costs (i.e., time

129

and effort) necessary to make the desired changes, and any budgetary considerations involved. If a strong enough case can be made for changing the objective(s), then you will probably need to go through a development process. This might entail having to negotiate subject-matter-resource support in order to put the new material together.

If the students feel that you did not adequately explain material in the training program, or if additional material needs to be provided to facilitate understanding of the concepts, this also may mean that additional resource time will be needed, but probably to a lesser extent than would be necessary if the objective changed completely. In this situation, you would be amending existing material rather than having to research, design, and create new information.

Similarly, if the information in the training program is found to be out of date, you should have relative ease in securing the support of resource personnel, unless, of course, the change entails a complete overhaul of what is currently being done. SMRs who are currently working in a particular area and are familiar with it should have little difficulty in looking at existing information and pinpointing the out-of-date areas. In many cases, this type of change can be handled by putting together a handout that compares the old versus the new information.

ENHANCE THE TRAINER'S SKILLS

In some training programs the evaluation results may indicate that one or more of the guest instructors needs to have his facilitation skills enhanced. This might involve one or more of the following actions:

☐ Working with the individual to improve his presentation skills. (For example, there may be some distracting mannerisms that affected how well the individual communicated the material.)

☐ Working with the individual to enhance key instructional technique skills. This, for example, might include providing additional information and opportunities to practice getting interim feedback (e.g., using questions during the session and during reviews of the program) so that he begins to feel more comfortable in being able to identify comprehension problems during the classroom session.

- [ ] Helping the individual construct a better measurement instrument by revising the current one or by building new testing devices

- [ ] Helping the person design a new (or better) demonstration/practice session so that students can better realize the consequences of their errors in a safe classroom environment

- [ ] Helping the individual develop or enhance various techniques that will better encourage peer-group learning

CHANGE INSTRUCTORS

For one reason or another, you may encounter a situation in which the only good alternative is to change guest instructors entirely. As you might expect, such a situation requires very careful and sensitive handling.

Even though an individual may be very competent technically in a particular area, he simply may not have the skills necessary to be an effective instructor. In such cases, providing this individual with additional train-the-trainer sessions will probably be ineffective. When this occurs, it is important that the problem be communicated promptly to the individual and agreement reached that it would be better for all people involved that a new instructor be found.

Although there is really no good way to handle the situation, a suggested approach would involve the following:

- [ ] Discuss the instructor's weaknesses (based upon the feedback data) with him and advise him that a new instructor will be sought for the next session. At this time it would also be appropriate to advise the individual that a summary of this discussion will be held with the individual's immediate supervisor.

- [ ] Hold a one-on-one discussion with the individual's manager, discuss the program's evaluations, provide a summary of the earlier meeting with the individual, and offer suggested corrective action.

☐ Encourage a three-way meeting with the manager and the guest instructor to again review the findings and construct an appropriate development plan. During this discussion, your role as program evaluator would be to serve as a resource to guarantee that there were no misunderstandings as to what occurred during the session and to offer development suggestions where appropriate.

No manager likes surprises. Let's assume for a moment that a process like this did not occur. The next time an instructor is needed from this manager's area, you go and ask for someone else. How do you respond to the manager's inquiry of, "Why don't you want _____ again?" You end up providing him with the same feedback, but the information is no longer fresh in your mind, and the manager may become annoyed—and rightfully so—because you did not bring this issue to his attention sooner. Because of this delay, the individual may have passed up some excellent development opportunities.

When taking any such action you need to use the utmost sensitivity and tact, both because personal egos are involved and because these same people may be asked to participate in the development of future programs. We talk more about giving feedback later in this section.

PROVIDE REMEDIAL WORK

Regardless of the problems with the training program or the instructor(s) involved, the principal burden of learning rests with the student. The bottom line is that the student has a responsibility to identify areas that she does not fully understand and to ask as many questions as necessary to get a clear answer. Unfortunately, very few students take this much effort to learn.

If the program objectives were accurate and the instructor was well qualified and able to explain the material, the source of the problem rests with the student's inability to understand or apply the concepts that were presented during the session. In such cases, some type of remedial work is necessary. This might consist of additional recommended reading materials, a suggestion to review selected portions of the material covered during the training session, counseling time for the individual, or enrollment of the person in a special training session with others who seem to be having a similar problem.

Ways to Give Constructive Feedback

It is easy for people to criticize the performance of others, especially with respect to a training program. It is not, however, easy to tell someone face-to-face in a helpful, constructive manner what problems were determined as a result of evaluations and what corrective action may be necessary.

Because we deal with personal egos, we sometimes prefer not to make waves in hopes that the problem will go away by itself. Unfortunately, this does not help anyone who is involved in the training program. The instructor suffers because he does not get good feedback and does not recognize a potential opportunity for professional growth. The student suffers because avenues for increased understanding are not made available to her. The guest instructor's manager is affected because he is shielded from knowing the development needs of his people.

When giving feedback, whether to a student or to a guest instructor, you should keep in mind certain considerations:

☐ *Base the feedback on factual data.* Very few people will argue with well-substantiated facts. If the feedback is based on observation, what was viewed should be documented and presented to the individual for comment. Feedback based on conjecture or information obtained through a third party (e.g., "I heard that you need to improve your interviewing skills") opens up room for denial and argument as to whether this problem actually exists or whether it is someone's biased judgment.

☐ *Ask questions to achieve a level of understanding.* You can learn more by having the individual respond to well-planned questions than by telling her all that is wrong and not providing an opportunity for rebuttal. The better an individual understands what problem has arisen and recognizes what alternative solutions are available, the more likely it is that she will accept the constructive criticism and be willing to do something about it.

133

☐ *Listen.* If an individual is provided an opportunity to respond to questions, listen to what is both said and not said. Sometimes the way answers are phrased or the tone of voice used can give important insight into how an individual really feels about a concern that has surfaced.

☐ *Provide positive reinforcement where necessary.* In only the rarest of situations will someone have done everything wrong. You can help build up an individual's confidence by reinforcing those things that he is doing well. It is very easy for an individual to feel that the criticism being discussed affects his entire work effort, when, in fact, it might only influence a small portion of it.

☐ *Have some realistic corrective measures in mind.* Before going into a feedback discussion, formulate some possible solutions to the problem that would be acceptable from a cost and time standpoint. If an individual is not able to determine what a good means for correcting her problem might be, then it will be your responsibility to provide possible alternative solutions. If you cannot think of any reasonable alternatives, then you need to reconsider whether to hold the discussion in the first place.

☐ *Communicate with the individual's manager.* Managers have a responsibility for the development of their employees. If you feel that the results of an evaluation point up areas of further development for an individual, this information should be made available to his manager. In this way, she can remain up-to-date on the strengths and weaknesses of her staff and can provide additional support in helping this individual's professional and personal growth.

SUMMARY

The task of training others is not an easy assignment, especially for those individuals, like yourself, who have to do it on a part-time basis and as an extension of their other technical job duties. As recently as the early 1970s, people were taught how to train others by the trial-and-error method. Basically, they were thrown into a room of people and told to train them. Needless to say, the use of this approach often produced mixed results.

The use of small-group activities at this time was limited. Lecture was felt to be the most effective way of training, and the instructor was considered to be *the* authority on the subject. Very few reference texts were available to help others learn how to train more effectively.

However, times have changed; and, fortunately, the attitudes and opinions about how training can be made more effective have improved. Instructional objectives are used to specify students' desired behavioral changes, trainers are permitted more latitude in how they can conduct their sessions, and technology has improved and can better support the needs of both the student and instructor. In addition, adult students have a better perception of why training is important and what is needed to enhance their personal and professional growth. This text was designed to provide some of the "survival" skills that you, the part-time trainer, should consider when designing, developing, conducting, and evaluating a training program. Because we only highlighted some of the key points in each area, you are also encouraged to seek out from the local library, corporate training facilities, and other similar sources additional reference materials that relate to each key topic, such as instructional techniques, presentation skills, and program evaluation.

In addition, we strongly encourage you to seek opportunities to give presentations, lead group sessions, and conduct other similar activities that can help you enhance your facilitation skills. Organizations such as Toastmasters, as well as local and national schools dedicated to teaching effective speaking techniques, are excellent resources for helping you build confidence in getting up before a group of people.

Demands of the business world today virtually require that an individual be adept at speaking in public, planning and facilitating meetings, and training others. Although this text has focused on "survival skills" within the context of training, you will find that these same skills apply to your running of meetings and your planning and conducting of business presentations.

These are the kinds of skills you never fully acquire, because all training sessions are different, and the technique that works in one training session may not work in another. You always have to think and be prepared for the unexpected. However, if you plan your session carefully, are knowledgeable about the various techniques and support equipment available, and have opportunities to practice and evaluate what you plan to do, then your chances of success in the training assignment are high.

Have a good session!

ADDITIONAL REFERENCES
AND MATERIALS

Volumes of information on training and presentation skills have been published. In your spare time you may wish to seek out some of these references in order to develop your ability in this field further. Many corporate training departments have these materials, or you can obtain them at public libraries or from the identified publishers.

BOOKS

Bradford, Leland P., ed. *Group Development*, La Jolla, Calif.: University Associates, 1974.

Broadwell, Martin M. *The Supervisor as an Instructor: A Guide for Classroom Training.* 4th ed. Reading, Mass.: Addison-Wesley Publishing Co., 1984.

Cooper, Susan, and Cathy Heenan. *Preparing, Designing, Leading Workshops: A Humanistic Approach.* Boston: CBI Publishing Co., 1980.

Doyle, Michael, and David Straus. *How to Make Meetings Work.* New York: Berkley Publishing Group, 1976.

Dyer, William G., ed. *Modern Theory and Method in Group Training.* New York: Van Nostrand Reinhold Co., 1972.

Edwards, Betty. *Drawing on the Right Side of the Brain.* Boston: Houghton Mifflin Co., 1979.

Frank, Milo. *How to Get Your Point Across in 30 Seconds—or Less.* New York: Simon & Schuster, 1986.

Gordon, Thomas. *Teacher Effectiveness Training.* New York: Peter H. Wyden, 1974.

Hays, Robert. *Practically Speaking—In Business, Industry and Government.* Reading, Mass.: Addison-Wesley Publishing Co., 1969.

Kemp, Jerrold E. *Planning and Producing Audiovisual Materials.* 2d ed. Scranton, Pa.: Chandler Publishing Co., 1968.

Knowles, Malcolm S. *Andragogy in Action.* San Francisco: Jossey-Bass Publishers, 1984.

_____. *The Modern Practice of Adult Education: From Pedagogy to Andragogy.* New York: Cambridge Book Co., 1980.

Loney, Glenn M. *Briefing and Conference Techniques.* New York: McGraw-Hill Book Co., 1959.

Mager, Robert F. *Measuring Instructional Results.* 2d ed. Belmont, Calif.: Pitman Learning, 1982.

_____. *Preparing Instructional Objectives*, 2d ed. Belmont, Calif.: Pitman Learning, 1980.

Morrisey, George L., and Thomas L. Sechrest. *Effective Business and Technical Presentations*. 3d ed. Reading, Mass.: Addison-Wesley Publishing Co., 1987.

Murray, Sheila L. *How to Organize and Manage a Seminar*. Englewood Cliffs, N.J.: Prentice-Hall, 1983.

Qubein, Nido R. *Communicate Like a Pro*. Englewood Cliffs, N.J.: Prentice-Hall, 1983.

Sanford, William P., and William H. Yeager. *Effective Business Speech*. New York: McGraw-Hill Book Co., 1960.

This, Leslie E., and Gordon L. Lippitt. *Learning Theories and Training*. Washington, D.C.: Leadership Resources, 1966.

Walter, Otis M., and Robert L. Scott. *Thinking and Speaking, A Guide to Intelligent Oral Communication*. New York: Macmillan Co., 1964.

PROGRAMS, MEDIA, AND OTHER MATERIAL

Anatomy of a Presentation, Roundtable Films. A film that illustrates what a novice presenter goes through in order to prepare for a presentation. The movie then shows the presentation and provides an opportunity for the viewer to critique it.

Effective Training Techniques by Martin M. Broadwell, Addison-Wesley Publishing Co. A three-videotape package that enables the learner to observe and practice various training techniques.

How to Write and Use Performance Objectives to Individualize Instruction by Robert E. Boston, Educational Technology Publications. A four-volume programmed-instruction text that guides the participant through the techniques of identifying and specifying training objectives.

Presentation Excellence with Walter Cronkite, CBS/Fox Video. A video-based learning system designed to help the learner understand, practice, and evaluate different instructional techniques.

Speak Up with Confidence with Jack Valenti, National Educational Media. A book and video program designed to make public speaking more enjoyable and productive.

CHECKLISTS AND WORKSHEETS
FOR EFFECTIVE
INSTRUCTIONAL PREPARATION

The purpose of these checklists and worksheets is to provide you with a set of reminders about the activities you need to consider when planning and facilitating a training program. If you are responsible for designing and facilitating an entire off-site training program, you will probably need to refer to most of the checklists/worksheets. On the other hand, if your responsibility is to conduct only one or more sessions, then you will need to refer only to certain portions of them. In addition, this is a general list of common training-preparation activities, and you should feel free to supplement or amend it, as appropriate, to meet your specific training needs.

For ease in using the checklists and worksheets, review them first to eliminate activities that do not apply to your situation. This can be done by putting "N/A" on the appropriate line. As you accomplish each of the other activities place an "X" on, or fill in the information on, the appropriate line. The result will be an excellent reference tool for you to determine readily what stage of development your training program is in.

Pre-Session Preparation

1. The overall goal of the training program is to _____
   _____.

2a. The specific learning objectives to be met are as follows (remember to use terms such as define, list, identify, analyze, etc.):
   A.

   B.

   C.

   D.

2b. Objectives have been signed-off by the client. Yes __ No __
   Date: _____

3a. The technique I will use to measure each of these objectives is

A.

B.

C.

D.

3b. Evaluation techniques have been signed off by client. Yes ___
No ___ Date: _____

4. What prerequisite knowledge and/or skills do the participants need to have prior to this session?

5. Who will be attending the session? (name and position title for each)

6. The person responsible for handling the following presession communication is:

Communication To:	Person Responsible
A. Management	_____
B. Program participants	_____
C. Subject-matter resources	_____
D. Other company personnel	_____

E. Training-site management   _____
(e.g., sales)

F. Site logistical personnel (e.g.,   _____
responsible for banquet set-
up, audiovisual equipment)

NOTE: If the training session is to be held off-site, see the additional checklist that follows.

7. The delivery date for the program is _____.

8. Training-room space has been reserved and confirmed.
Yes ___ No ___ Date: _____

With Whom: _____

9a. Subject-matter-resource support will be needed to meet the
following objectives of the training program:
A.

B.

C.

D.

9b. The following SMRs will be made available to conduct this
training, and their attendance has been requested and confirmed.

	SMR's Name	Date Requested	Date Confirmed
A.	_____	_____	_____
B.	_____	_____	_____
C.	_____	_____	_____
D.	_____	_____	_____

10a. The training program will require the following training materials to be ordered from vendors:

Material Needed	Vendor	Quantity	Date Ordered	Date Received
A. _____	_____	_____	_____	_____
B. _____	_____	_____	_____	_____
C. _____	_____	_____	_____	_____
D. _____	_____	_____	_____	_____

10b. The person responsible for ordering these materials is

Material	Responsible Person
A. _____	_____
B. _____	_____
C. _____	_____
D. _____	_____

11a. The training program agenda has been developed.
Yes ___ No ___ Date: _____

11b. The agenda has been approved by client. Yes ___

No ___ Date: _____

By whom: _____

11c. The agenda has been communicated to
A. Management: Yes ___ No ___ Date: _____

B. SMRs: Yes ___ No ___ Date: _____

C. Other necessary company personnel: Yes ___

No ___ Date: _____

Persons (identify by title): _____

12a. Invitation letters have been sent to program participants:

Yes ___ No ___

Date sent to participants: _____

12b. The invitation letters included the following information:
   A. Program dates: Yes ___ No ___

   B. Start and end times: Yes ___ No ___

   C. Dress requirements: Yes ___ No ___

   D. Transportation data and requirements: Yes ___ No ___

   E. Pocket-money needs: Yes ___ No ___

   F. Additional items of importance (identify):
      ☐ _____ Yes ___ No ___
      ☐ _____ Yes ___ No ___

13a. Rooming arrangements have been completed and confirmed for the following attendees, SMRs, management guests, consultants, facilitators, and/or program coordinators:

Name	Single/ Double Occupancy	Smoking/ No Smoking	Male/ Female	Length of Stay	Date Confirmed

13b. Rooming list has been sent to hotel. Yes ___ No ___
   Date: _____

   NOTE: This should be done a minimum of two weeks prior to the start of the training session.

14. The following training material and supplies are required for this program:

Material/ Supplies	Quantity	3-Hole Punched	Date Ordered	Date Rec'd	Responsibility

148

15. Completion certificates, final exams, etc., have been removed from the packaged text material. Yes ___ No ___

    Date: _____

16a. The following special equipment (e.g., CRTs) is needed for the program and has been ordered and received:

Equipment	Quantity	Date Ordered	Date Installed	Test OK?	Person Responsible

16b. Arrangements have been made for dismantling special equipment and returning to vendor. Yes ___ No ___

    Date: _____ To be picked up on: _____

CONFERENCE CENTER WORKSHEET

OFF-SITE ARRANGEMENTS

1. Meeting Date: _____ Contact: _____

   Telephone: _____

2. Key Facility Staff

Manager _____ Extension _____

Banquet _____ Extension _____

Audiovisual
Equipment _____ Extension _____

Front Desk _____ Extension _____

Engineering _____ Extension _____

Bell Captain _____ Extension _____

3. *Food Arrangements*

Event	Confirmed Number	Special Arrangements (podium, mike, seating)
Breakfast	_____	_____
A.M. Break	_____	_____
Lunch	_____	_____
P.M. Break	_____	_____
Dinner	_____	_____

4. *Meeting-Room Arrangements*

Session	Number of Attendees	Seating Arrangement*	Special Needs**

*Indicate whether room is to be arranged with rectangular or circular tables and the number at each table. For example, the notation 4R6 might mean you want to have four round tables with six people at each. Similarly, the notation 2R-U could mean two people at each rectangular table with the tables in a U-shape.

**Used to indicate special visual-aid needs such as an overhead projector, videotape camera, as well as a podium, changes in room configuration, etc.

5. Rooming Arrangements

Name	Single/ Double Occupancy	Smoking/ No Smoking	Male/ Female	Check In	Check Out	Special Needs

6. Billing Arrangements

A. A master bill has been set up to cover:

☐ Room and tax: Yes ___ No ___

☐ Incidental expenses (valet, telephone): Yes ___ No ___

B. Attendees will be responsible for all charges at checkout.

7. Breakfast, Lunch, and Dinner Menus

Attach separate sheet to specify what meal selections have been made for each day of the training session and any special dietary requirements that may apply to, or been specified by, individual attendees.

8. Special Arrangements

Event	Arrangement/Time

A. Check in of attendees

B. Checkout

Event	Arrangement/Time

C. Preconference meeting with
site staff*

D. Special functions**

  *It is suggested that you meet with the management staff of the training site a maximum of two days prior to the start of your session. This will enable you to discuss your agenda with them and work out any special details or arrangements.

  **Special functions would include special arrangements (e.g., outdoor barbecue, tennis or golf tournament, after-dinner dance)

PRESENTATION/FACILITATION PREPARATION

1. The training room and breakout room(s), where applicable, are ready for use:

  ☐ Room temperature comfortable? Yes ___ No ___

  ☐ Light switches located? Yes ___ No ___

  ☐ Power outlets operating? Yes ___ No ___

  ☐ Projection screens located and operating?

    Yes ___ No ___ Not needed ___

  ☐ Seating arrangement appropriate? Yes ___ No ___

2. The following reference material will be needed for use during the training program:

Reference Material	Current? (Y/N)	Date Ordered	Date Rec'd	Responsibility

3. The following visual aids are needed for use during the program:

Visual Aid	When Needed	Can Operate (Y/N)	Person Responsible for Obtaining

4. Materials and supplies are available in sufficient quantities and ready for use:

- ☐ Handout material in desired form (three-hole punched, collated, etc.): Yes ____ No ____

- ☐ Reference materials: Yes ____ No ____

- ☐ Training aids (charts, reports, diagrams, etc.): Yes ____ No ____

5. Training notes and lesson plans:

- ☐ are organized for quick reference and will allow for a smooth transition between subjects and/or activities: Yes ____ No ____

- ☐ define the objectives to be accomplished, the technique to be used, the content to be communicated, and the time allowance for each program segment: Yes ____ No ____

6. Program attendees, SMRs and guests:

- ☐ Background information on audience members has been obtained in order to identify both potential "friendly faces" and problem personalities: Yes ____ No ____

☐ Participants have tent cards and/or lapel tags to facilitate personal identification: Yes ___ No ___

☐ Meetings have been held with all guest speakers to discuss the objectives they are to accomplish, provide background information on what has been discussed prior to their presentations, and give an overview of the audience: Yes ___ No ___.

☐ SMR personnel are standing by to answer questions or assist with problems: Yes ___ No ___

7. You have practiced all intended demonstrations and are comfortable with your ability to handle most problems that may arise? Yes ___ No ___

PERSONAL PREPARATION

1. Your attire is appropriate for the meeting setting: Yes ___ No ___

2. Your personal appearance reflects the professional image you want to portray: Yes ___ No ___

3. You have reviewed your notes and lesson plans have been reviewed so that you feel comfortable with the material being presented and the order of presentation: Yes ___ No ___

4. You have rehearsed the techniques planned for use during the first five minutes of your session, and you are very satisfied with them: Yes ___ No ___

5. You do not feel the need to make excuses for yourself, the material being presented, the training session's objectives, or the meeting site: Yes ___ No ___

6. You are aware of what material has been discussed prior to your session (particularly important where more than one speaker is involved in a training session): Yes ___ No ___

7. You feel you are as ready as you will ever be! Yes ___ No ___

IN-SESSION POINTS

1. You have confirmed with site management the number of attendees for lunch and dinner: Yes ___ No ___

2. Requests for unplanned special meal arrangements have been communicated to site management: Yes ___ No ___

3. Need for access to, and/or availability of, additional subject-matter resources and materials has been identified and the resources secured: Yes ___ No ___

4. Agenda adjustments have been made to compensate for time over- or underruns. (NOTE: Massive changes that significantly affect the attainment of the program's objectives, the speaking schedules of outside resource persons, or access to special equipment should be carefully considered and signed off by the client prior to implementation):
   Yes ___ No ___

5. You have made site management aware of inoperative equipment, problems with environmental conditions (e.g., meeting room too cold), and/or inadequate attention to service details:
   Yes ___ No ___

POSTSESSION POINTS

1. The following people (both on- and off-site) should receive thank-you notes for their help and cooperation during the training session:

Name	Manager	Date Sent

2. Evaluation and Feedback

☐ Participant-feedback questionnaires have been analyzed to determine the strengths and weaknesses in the program: Yes ___ No ___

☐ Follow-up evaluations have been conducted (maximum of six months after training has been completed) and results communicated to management: Yes ___ No ___

☐ Training program material and/or agenda has been amended to reflect results of the postsession evaluation: Yes ___ No ___

☐ Constructive criticism given to guest speakers as well as relevant feedback obtained from the evaluations: Yes ___ No ___

3. Manager of SMR has been contacted, and his or her permission received, in order to get SMR's continued assistance in updating program content or support materials as appropriate: Yes ___ No ___